MASTER THE
NEW YORK CITY
SPECIALIZED
HIGH SCHOOLS
ADMISSIONS
TEST

7th Edition

Stephen Krane

About Peterson's

Peterson's provides the accurate, dependable, high-quality education content and guidance you need to succeed. No matter where you are on your academic or professional path, you can rely on Peterson's print and digital publications for the most up-to-date education exploration data, expert test-prep tools, and top-notch career success resources—everything you need to achieve your goals.

For more information, contact Peterson's, 3 Columbia Circle, Suite 205, Albany, NY 12203-5158; 800-338-3282 Ext. 54229; or find us online at www.petersonsbooks.com.

Visit us online at www.petersonsbooks.com and let Peterson's help you achieve your goals.

By printing this book on recycled paper (40% post-consumer waste) 36 trees were saved.

Certified Chain of Custody

60% Certified Fiber Sourcing and
40% Post-Consumer Recycled

www.sfiprogram.org

*This label applies to the text stock.

Sustainability—Its Importance to Peterson's

What does sustainability mean to Peterson's? As a leading publisher, we are aware that our business has a direct impact on vital resources—most especially the trees that are used to make our books. Peterson's is proud that its products are certified to the Sustainable Forestry Initiative (SFI) chain-of-custody standard and that all of its books are printed on paper that is 40 percent post-consumer waste using vegetable-based ink.

Being a part of the Sustainable Forestry Initiative (SFI) means that all of out vendors—from paper suppliers to printers—have undergone rigorous audits to demonstrate that they are maintaining a sustainable environment.

Peterson's continuously strives to find new ways to incorporate sustainability throughout all aspects of its business.

Contents

APPENDIX

Before You Begin

HOW THIS BOOK IS ORGANIZED

You want to do your best on this test and that's why you bought this book. Used correctly, this self-tutor will show you what to expect while giving you the most effective practice with subjects you can expect to see on the actual exam. *Master the New York City Specialized High Schools Admissions Test* provides you with the necessary tools to make the most of the study time you have, including:

- **"Top 10 Ways to Raise Your Score"** gives you test-taking strategies.

- **Part I** provides the basics of the New York City Specialized High Schools Admissions Test.

- **Part II** includes 10 "mini" practice tests followed by detailed answer explanations.

- The **Appendix** includes bonus information about, and two practice tests for, the Hunter College High School Entrance Examination.

SPECIAL STUDY FEATURES

Master the New York City Specialized High Schools Admissions Test is designed to be user-friendly. To this end, it includes several features to make your preparation much more efficient.

Overview

Each chapter begins with a bulleted overview, listing the topics to be covered in the chapter. This will allow you to quickly target the areas in which you are most interested.

Summing It Up

Each chapter ends with a point-by-point summary that captures the most important points contained in the chapter. They are a convenient way to review key points. As you work your way through the book, keep your eye on the margins to find bonus information and advice. Information can be found in the following forms:

Tip

Tips provide valuable strategies for raising your score.

Practice Tests

Each practice test is designed to help students prepare with little anxiety. While the actual test contains 95 questions, we believe that the format of our 10 reduced practice tests gives students ample opportunities to succeed without stress. Each test can be completed in 1 hour.

YOU'RE WELL ON YOUR WAY TO SUCCESS

Master the New York City Specialized High Schools Admissions Test will prepare you for the test you need to attend the high school of your choice. Good luck!

GIVE US YOUR FEEDBACK

We welcome any comments or suggestions you may have about this publication. Please call our customer service department at 800-338-3282 ext. 54229 or send an email message to custsvc@petersons.com. Your feedback will help us make educational dreams possible for you—and others like you.

TOP 10 WAYS TO RAISE YOUR SCORE

When it comes to taking the SHSAT, some test-taking skills will do you more good than others. Here are our picks for the top 10 ways to raise your score.

1. **Get to the test center early.** Make sure you give yourself plenty of extra time to get there.

2. **Listen to the test monitors and follow their instructions carefully.**

3. **Read every word of the instructions. Read every word of every question.**

4. **Mark your answers by completely darkening the answer space of your choice.**

5. **Mark only ONE answer for each question, even if you think that more than one answer is correct.** You must choose only one. If you mark more than one answer, the scoring machine will consider you wrong.

6. **If you change your mind, completely erase your initial choice.** Leave no doubt as to which answer you intend.

7. **Check often to be sure that the question number matches the answer space, that you haven't skipped a space by mistake.**

8. **Stay alert.** Be careful not to mark a wrong answer just because you weren't concentrating.

9. **Don't panic.** If you cannot finish a part before time is up, don't worry. Do not let your performance on any one part affect your performance on any other part.

10. **Check and recheck, time permitting.** If you finish a part before time is up, use the remaining time to check that each question is answered in the right space and that there is only one answer for each question. Return to the questions you found difficult and rethink them.

PART I

THE NEW YORK CITY SPECIALIZED HIGH SCHOOLS ADMISSIONS TEST (SHSAT)

All About the New York City Specialized High Schools

chapter 1

OVERVIEW

- **The specialized high schools**
- **The Specialized High School Admissions Test (SHSAT)**
- **Summer discovery program**
- **Summing it up**

THE SPECIALIZED HIGH SCHOOLS

There are eight specialized high schools that require an entrance exam according to the 2012-2013 Specialized High Schools Student Handbook. These are Bronx High School of Science; Brooklyn Technical High School; Brooklyn Latin School; High School for Mathematics, Science and Engineering at City College; High School of American Studies at Lehman College; Queens High School for the Sciences at York College; Staten Island Technical High School; and Stuyvesant High School. Specialized high schools are public high schools established and run by the New York City Board of Education to serve the needs of academically gifted students. New York State Education Law makes a written examination a requirement for admission to these high schools. Places are awarded to those students who earn the highest scores on the entrance exam, the New York City Specialized High Schools Admissions Test (SHSAT).

Although each of the specialized high schools has its own unique features, all seven emphasize mathematics and science, offering many intriguing electives and a wide range of advanced placement courses. Of course, each school also offers all the basic New York State-required academic courses that every student needs for success in college and beyond.

The exciting and academically challenging atmosphere of the specialized high schools stimulates both the students and the teachers. Enrichment courses are available in the humanities as well as in the sciences and technology.

THE SPECIALIZED HIGH SCHOOLS ADMISSIONS TEST (SHSAT)

The New York City Specialized High Schools Admissions Test is offered to all eighth- and ninth-grade students residing within the five boroughs of New York City who wish to attend one of the specialized high schools. The same examination is given for all seven schools and students who qualify may attend the school of their choice. The qualifying score, however, depends upon the number of seats available and the scores of all candidates. The tests are graded and arranged in order of rank, from the highest score to the lowest score. Each school has a number of freshman and sophomore seats to fill, and seats are filled starting with the highest test scores. When all available seats have been filled, the cutoff mark is determined.

Students who miss the cutoff score of their first-choice school may be assigned to their second-choice school if their score is above the cutoff for that school. This procedure continues until all seats in all seven schools have been filled.

Eighth and ninth grade students in public, private, and parochial schools who are NYC residents planning on attending the specialized high schools of NYC must take the Specialized High Schools Admission Test. The testing sites are set so that students sitting for the test will take the exam in the geographic area where their home is located.

The exam is given in late October typically at a specialized high school or other local public high school in order to make it convenient for the candidates to travel to the test site.

It is very important that a student planning to take the exam see his or her guidance counsellor in September to register to take the exam. All candidates will be given a booklet written by the Board of Education of NYC entitled: *Specialized High Schools Student Handbook*, which contains all of the current dates and locations for the exam. The handbook is also available online. It is essential that you have this handbook.

SUMMER DISCOVERY PROGRAM

The specialized high schools offer a Summer Discovery Program for students who have come close to the cutoff number and have been recommended by a school counselor. To be eligible for this program, a student must also meet any one of the following criteria:

- be from a Chapter 1 school and be eligible for food services; or
- be receiving public assistance; or
- come from a family whose income is below the Department of Social Services' standards; or
- be a ward of the state or a foster child; or
- have entered the United States within the last four years and live in a home where English is not the language spoken.

Students accepted in to the Summer Discovery Program who are successful in passing the courses will become students at the school where they were conditionally accepted.

SUMMING IT UP

- The specialized high schools are: Bronx High School of Science; Brooklyn Technical High School; High School for Mathematics, Science and Engineering at City College; High School of American Studies at Lehman College; Queens High School for the Sciences at York College; Staten Island Technical High School; and Stuyvesant High School.

- You are expected to bring an admission ticket to the test center on the day of the test.

- Tests are graded and arranged in order of rank, from the highest score to the lowest score. The freshman and sophomore seats are filled starting with the highest test scores.

All About the SHSAT

OVERVIEW

- Timetable for test-takers
- Exam format
- Scoring the exam
- Verbal sample questions and explanations
- Mathematics sample questions and explanations
- Summing it up

The SHSAT is a difficult test. It is intended to assess the verbal and mathematical skills required for success at a high school for academically gifted students.

The best preparation for the test is to keep up with your schoolwork throughout the year. You can, however, help to increase your verbal skills through independent reading of a variety of books, magazines, and newspapers. And you can build needed math skills by solving additional problems—particularly challenging problems that go beyond what you do in your mathematics class.

The ten mini-exams in Part II of this book are designed to give you practice with the type of questions you will be expected to answer when you take the actual SHSAT. Taking these practice tests will give you the confidence-building experience you need to score high on your test and get into the specialized high school of your choice.

chapter 2

NOTE

Before taking the SHSAT, you must sign a statement indicating that you are well enough to take the test.

TIMETABLE FOR TEST-TAKERS

September/early October: | Students should be given specific information about the Specialized High Schools along with an application.

Late October/Early November: | The site of the exam is dependent on the geographic location of the school they are currently attending.

February: | Students are notified of their scores and must accept or reject the seat offered if they were successful.

September next: | Students begin attendance at the specialized high school.

EXAM FORMAT

The actual Specialized High Schools Admissions Test is 2 hours and 30 minutes long and consists of 95 multiple-choice questions. The format of the latest examination is as follows:

Part I. Verbal (45 questions)—75 minutes consisting of:

   5 Scrambled Paragraphs questions

  10 Logical Reasoning questions

  30 Reading Comprehension questions (5 reading passages with 6 questions on each)

Part II. Mathematics (50 questions)—75 minutes consisting of:

     Quantitative Comparison questions, and Problem Solving questions

Handling the Time Allowed

You can break up the 150 minutes of test time as best suits you. The test is designed to take about 75 minutes for each section, so don't stay on the verbal section longer than 75 minutes. Each of the five Scrambled Paragraphs questions has twice the score value, compared to all of the other questions on the test. When you hit the 75-minute mark, move on to the math section. If you finish the math section before time runs out, you can go back to any unanswered questions in the verbal section.

Don't get bogged down on any one question. Instead, mark a difficult question with a question mark and go back to it later, if time allows. Concentrate, read every word, answer the question or skip it, and *move on*.

Marking Your Answer Choices

The exam questions are answered by filling in the appropriate circles on a separate answer sheet. You will need to bring at least two number-2 pencils to mark your answer sheet—and a *good eraser* in case you need to change an answer. It's also helpful to bring a watch to keep track of the time. The proctors will put the time on the board, but not on a minute-by-minute basis.

You will be given scratch paper for figuring out problems in logical reasoning and mathematics. You are also allowed to write in the test booklet as you work out solutions to the problems. No calculators are allowed for this exam.

All test questions have either four or five options to choose from. In each case, only one is correct. If you fill in more than one answer for any question, you will be marked wrong for that question; therefore, if you wish to change an answer, you must erase your first answer completely before filling in your new answer choice.

SCORING THE EXAM

Since there is no penalty for guessing on the SHSAT, you should answer every question. Educated guessing involves eliminating answer choices you know are wrong and then guessing from the choices that remain. Each time you eliminate an answer choice as wrong, you increase your chances of selecting the correct answer for that question.

Your final score is determined by the number of correct answers you have chosen. Three scores will be reported to the school where you took your test: your Verbal score, your Math score, and your Composite score (the sum of your verbal and math scores). Your composite score is the score that is used to determine admission to a specialized high school.

VERBAL SAMPLE QUESTIONS AND EXPLANATIONS

Following are samples of each kind of question you will find on the SHSAT, along with suggestions for solving each one.

Scrambled Paragraphs

Directions: The paragraph below consists of six sentences in scrambled order. The first, or topic, sentence is given, and you are to arrange the rest in an order that makes sense, each sentence following from the one before in that it explains the earlier sentence or adds to it.

Write the numbers to the left of the letters (in pencil so you can change them as often as you need). When you are satisfied, mark your choices on the answer sheet.

Because you get no partial credit for having only some of the sentences in a paragraph in order and because trying different arrangements to find which reads best requires more time than other test questions, each of the scrambled paragraphs carries twice the weight of other questions on the test.

Q In legend, books, and movies, Americans have tended to romanticize the pirates who roamed the seas from ancient days, most famously from the sixteenth through the eighteenth centuries.

_____**Q.** If they didn't die from disease, they were captured and sentenced to death by the authorities.

_____**R.** To make matters even worse, often they were killed or marooned by their own crews.

_____**S.** Many of them became pirates because of the hard life of a sailor, while others just liked the adventure and the possibility of vast riches (which few achieved).

_____**T.** They were a mostly loutish, ill-kempt bunch, usually drunk and quarrelsome.

_____**U.** In actuality, however, their lives were neither swashbuckling, nor were the pirates nearly as dashing as they have been portrayed.

The second sentence is Ⓠ Ⓡ Ⓢ Ⓣ Ⓤ

The third sentence is Ⓠ Ⓡ Ⓢ Ⓣ Ⓤ

The fourth sentence is Ⓠ Ⓡ Ⓢ Ⓣ Ⓤ

The fifth sentence is Ⓠ Ⓡ Ⓢ Ⓣ Ⓤ

The sixth sentence is Ⓠ Ⓡ Ⓢ Ⓣ Ⓤ

A The correct order is USTQR.

U If they didn't die from disease, they were captured and sentenced to death by the authorities.

S To make matters even worse, often they were killed or marooned by their own crews.

T Many of them became pirates because of the hard life of a sailor, while others just liked the adventure and the possibility of vast riches (which few achieved).

Q They were a mostly loutish, ill-kempt bunch, usually drunk and quarrelsome.

R In actuality, however, their lives were neither swashbuckling, nor were the pirates nearly as dashing as they have been portrayed.

Logical Reasoning

Directions: Read each question very carefully and choose the **best** answer from the five choices given. Select your answer based **only** on the information provided.

You will probably need to make a diagram to solve the problem. Be particularly careful in your interpretation of such words as *between, above, below, before,* and *after.* For example, "The oak tree is between two maples" doesn't mean that the oak tree is the only thing between the two maples. One or more other trees may also be found between the two maples.

Q Five different colored blocks of equal size and shape are stacked on top of each other. The red block is between the blue and green blocks. The yellow block is above the green block and is not an end block. The purple block is farthest from the yellow block and is not the bottom block. What color is the top block?

    (F) Blue

    (G) Yellow

    (H) Purple

    (J) Green

    (K) It cannot be determined from the information given.

A **The correct answer is (H).** Read the problem through carefully. Then, starting with the first bit of information, draw the diagrams that satisfy each condition. "The red block is between the blue and green blocks" [see Step 1].

"The yellow block is above the green block and is not an end block" [see Step 2]. There are four places where yellow can go. Two of these places must have purple above so that yellow won't be an end block.

"The purple block is farthest from the yellow block and is not the bottom block." This statement leaves you with only one of the five choices [see Step 3], so (H) is the only correct choice.

Step 1	Step 2	Step 3
B *or* G	P *or* P	P
R R	Y – –Y	B
G B	B G	R
	Y–	Y
	R R	G
	Y–	
	G B	

Q Bill is John's son by John's first marriage. Bill's dad is currently married to Joan, his second wife. Joan's younger sister Betty is married to Bill. John is Betty's

(A) stepfather and uncle-in-law.

(B) stepbrother and stepfather.

(C) natural father and stepbrother.

(D) father-in-law and brother-in-law.

(E) uncle by marriage.

A **The correct answer is (D).** Start by making a diagram of the relationships. First, place John in a circle above Bill and connect them by a line indicating the father-son relationship.

(1)

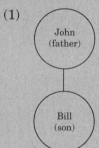

Next, put Joan in a circle next to John and connect these two circles with a line indicating that John and Joan are husband and wife.

(2)

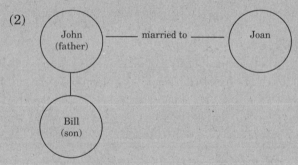

Now add Betty under Joan with a connecting line indicating that they are sisters. Draw another line from Betty to Bill to indicate that they are husband and wife.

(3)

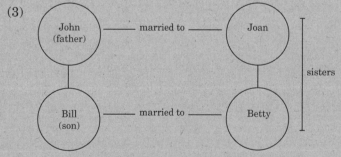

Now you can see that John is Betty's father-in-law, because she is married to his son. But John is also Betty's brother-in-law, because she is the sister of John's wife.

Reading Comprehension

Directions: Read the passage below and answer the questions that follow. Remember to **use only the information you have read in the passage** when answering the questions; you may reread the passage if necessary.

QUESTIONS 4–7 ARE BASED ON THE FOLLOWING PASSAGE.

Michelangelo, one of the greatest artists of all time, was a sculptor, painter, and architect. Born in Italy in 1475, he was still a child when it became evident that he had a special gift. He was encouraged to attend several fine art schools, which were supported by the Catholic Church and wealthy patrons of art. There he developed his skills and soon became one of the great Italian artists of his day, achieving eminence while still a young man.

In 1508, Michelangelo was commissioned by the Pope to paint the ceiling of the Sistine Chapel. This enormous undertaking took four years of passionate work, and Michelangelo covered the ceiling with paintings that depict scenes from the Bible.

Much of Michelangelo's work was supported by the heads of the Catholic Church. His art, as you would assume, has religious significance. Michelangelo's magnificent statue of David, his Madonna, and his Moses are but a few examples of the well-known religious figures he depicted in his works of art. Saint Peter's Basilica was his last and greatest architectural achievement. This monumental temple is in Vatican City, Rome. People of all faiths are drawn to Italy to view this masterpiece as well as Michelangelo's sculptures and paintings.

Q Which of the following best summarizes what the passage is mainly about?

(F) Famous Italian art

(G) Michelangelo, his life and times

(H) The significance of religion in art

(J) The art of Michelangelo

(K) Michelangelo, the man

A The correct answer is (J). The entire passage deals with the art of Michelangelo. Choice (F) is easily dismissed, while choices (G), (H), and (K) may cause you to think for a moment. But choices (G) and (K), which are about Michelangelo, are not specifically about his art. The significance of religion in art, choice (H), is only touched upon and is not the major topic of the passage.

Q Michelangelo's great artistic talents

   (A) kept him painting throughout his life.

   (B) are seen in paintings, architecture, and sculpture.

   (C) never gave him time for a normal life.

   (D) made him very religious.

   (E) were superior when compared to those of today's artists.

A The correct answer is (B). The first paragraph states that Michelangelo was a great painter, architect, and sculptor; the rest of the passage describes examples of his work in each area. Choices (C), (D), and (E) are not discussed, and choice (A) is an inference you can't really make from what is stated in the passage.

Q Which of the following does the passage imply about Michelangelo's artistic skills?

   (F) They were self-taught, upgraded, and polished through hard work and self-criticism.

   (G) They needed only minor refinements.

   (H) They were refined at public art schools.

   (J) They were taught by the church.

   (K) They were developed at special schools supported by the church.

A The correct answer is (K). The first paragraph states in very similar words that the church supported the schools where Michelangelo developed his skills. Choice (F) sounds good but does not follow from the passage. Choices (G) and (H) are wrong and easily dismissed. Choice (J) is a little tricky but wrong in that the church didn't teach art skills.

Q Which of the following is given as a specific example of Michaelangelo's great talent as a sculptor?

   (A) The ceiling of the Sistine Chapel

   (B) The works depicting Moses

   (C) His portrayal of the biblical figure of David

   (D) His being supported in fine arts schools

   (E) Saint Peter's Basilica

A The correct answer is (C). Paragraph three specifically states that the statue of David was one of Michelangelo's great well-known religious works of art. The other choices are wrong because none is an example of Michelangelo's talent as a sculptor. Choice (B), which mentions Moses, may give you a second thought, but if you read paragraph three carefully, it doesn't say Moses was a sculpture—just a work of art.

MATHEMATICS SAMPLE QUESTIONS AND EXPLANATIONS

The mathematics portion of the SHSAT contains problems in algebra , geometry, probability, and statistics. The basics of these problems come from an outline provided by the New York State Education Department. The publication is called, *NYSED Mathematics Resource Guide with Core Curriculum*. It is available online from the New York State Department of Education website: www.nysed.gov.

The publication is only an outline, basics are included and terminology is present but the SHSAT does go beyond what would have been learned in grades 1-7 (1-8 for ninth graders). Since the test is designed to identify intellectually gifted students many of the questions will go beyond the basics.

The questions in the ten mini-tests presented in this book will help you prepare for the test. It is also helpful to practice on the past tests in the Specialized High School's Handbook. Further study by doing challenging problems in a math text will also sharpen your skills.

Formulas and symbol definitions will likely not be included in the actual exam. A list of common formulas and symbols in the following ten practice tests are there for you to memorize. This list will not be available when you take the actual exam.

The overwhelming majority of the problems need to be worked out on paper. Work neatly and carefully; you don't want to get a wrong answer because you missed a step in your calculations. Only after carefully reading a problem should you begin to solve it.

Problem Solving

Directions: For each question, solve the problem and select the best answer from the choices given.

Q $-8 + (-4) - (-3) =$

(A) -15

(B) 15

(C) -9

(D) 9

(E) 1

A The correct answer is (C).

$-8 + (-4) - (-3) =$

$-12 - (-3) =$

$-12 + \quad 3 = -9$

(To subtract, change the subtraction sign and add.)

Q If a certain ice cream sells for $7.60 a gallon, what is the cost of a pint of this ice cream?

   (F) $3.80

   (G) $6.08

   (H) $1.90

   (J) $9.50

   (K) $0.95

A **The correct answer is (K).** There are 8 pints in a gallon.

$$\begin{array}{r} .95 \\ 8\overline{)7.60} \\ -72 \\ \hline 40 \\ -40 \\ \hline 00 \end{array}$$

This problem can be solved quickly by looking over the answers and saying to yourself, $7.60 is just under $8.00, so a pint costs under $1.00. The only answer choice under $1.00 is (K).

Q If 3 yards of cloth cost x dollars, then what is the cost of 2 yards of this cloth?

   (A) $\dfrac{2x}{3}$

   (B) $\dfrac{3x}{2}$

   (C) $2x$

   (D) $\dfrac{x}{2}$

   (E) $\dfrac{x}{3}$

A **The correct answer is (A).** Three yards cost x dollars; therefore, 1 yard costs $\dfrac{x}{3}$.

Two yards would then be $\dfrac{x}{3} \times 2$ or $\dfrac{2x}{3}$.

Q The larger acute angle in a right triangle is 2 times the measure of the smaller acute angle. The number of degrees in the smaller angle is:

(F) 60

(G) 90

(H) 45

(J) 30

(K) 15

A **The correct answer is (J).** A right triangle has one 90° angle, and the sum of the angles of a triangle equals 180°. Therefore, the sum of the two acute angles equals 90°. Since one acute angle is two times the measure of the other:

$$2x + x = 90$$
$$3x = 90$$
$$x = 30 \, (\text{smaller acute angle})$$

Q

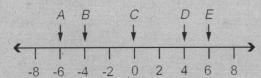

How would you move along the number line above to find the difference between −6 and 4?

(A) From *E* to *B*

(B) From *A* to *D*

(C) From *B* to *D*

(D) From *D* to *A*

(E) From *B* to *E*

A **The correct answer is (B).** To find the difference, we subtract −6 from 4 and move from −6 to 4, a distance of +10 units.

Q How many sixths are there in $\frac{4}{5}$?

(F) $2\frac{3}{8}$

(G) 3

(H) $4\frac{4}{5}$

(J) $5\frac{1}{5}$

(K) 6

A **The correct answer is (H).** Simply divide $\frac{4}{5}$ by $\frac{1}{6}$ to find the answer.

$$\frac{4}{5} \div \frac{1}{6} = \frac{4}{5} \bullet \frac{6}{1} = \frac{24}{5} = 4\frac{4}{5}$$

Q Four games drew an average of 36,500 people per game. If the attendance at the first three games was 32,000, 35,500, and 38,000, how may people attended the fourth game?

(A) 36,500

(B) 37,000

(C) 39,000

(D) 40,500

(E) 43,000

A **The correct answer is (D).** Four games averaging 36,500 people per game total 146,000 people in attendance. The total for the first three games was 105,500. The fourth game attracted 40,500 people.

SUMMING IT UP

- The SHSAT assesses verbal and math skills.
- The verbal section includes Scrambled Paragraphs, Logical Reasoning, and Reading Comprehension.
- The mathematics section includes algebra, geometry, probability, and statistics.

PART II

TEN PRACTICE TESTS

Practice Tests 1–10

The ten practice tests that follow are composed of the kinds of questions included on the actual exam. However, these practice tests have been proportionally reduced in length so that you can take and correct an entire test in about an hour. You will improve with each test you take as you review your mistakes and learn how to handle the questions.

Each practice test is 40 minutes long and contains 13 verbal and 13 math questions.

ANSWER SHEET PRACTICE TEST 1
Part I: Verbal

Scrambled Paragraphs

Paragraph 1

The second sentence is Ⓠ Ⓡ Ⓢ Ⓣ Ⓤ

The third sentence is Ⓠ Ⓡ Ⓢ Ⓣ Ⓤ

The fourth sentence is Ⓠ Ⓡ Ⓢ Ⓣ Ⓤ

The fifth sentence is Ⓠ Ⓡ Ⓢ Ⓣ Ⓤ

The sixth sentence is Ⓠ Ⓡ Ⓢ Ⓣ Ⓤ

Paragraph 2

The second sentence is Ⓠ Ⓡ Ⓢ Ⓣ Ⓤ

The third sentence is Ⓠ Ⓡ Ⓢ Ⓣ Ⓤ

The fourth sentence is Ⓠ Ⓡ Ⓢ Ⓣ Ⓤ

The fifth sentence is Ⓠ Ⓡ Ⓢ Ⓣ Ⓤ

The sixth sentence is Ⓠ Ⓡ Ⓢ Ⓣ Ⓤ

Logical Reasoning

3. Ⓐ Ⓑ Ⓒ Ⓓ Ⓔ
4. Ⓕ Ⓖ Ⓗ Ⓙ Ⓚ
5. Ⓐ Ⓑ Ⓒ Ⓓ Ⓔ

Reading

6. Ⓕ Ⓖ Ⓗ Ⓙ Ⓚ
7. Ⓐ Ⓑ Ⓒ Ⓓ Ⓔ
8. Ⓕ Ⓖ Ⓗ Ⓙ Ⓚ
9. Ⓐ Ⓑ Ⓒ Ⓓ Ⓔ
10. Ⓕ Ⓖ Ⓗ Ⓙ Ⓚ
11. Ⓐ Ⓑ Ⓒ Ⓓ Ⓔ
12. Ⓕ Ⓖ Ⓗ Ⓙ Ⓚ
13. Ⓐ Ⓑ Ⓒ Ⓓ Ⓔ

PART II: MATHEMATICS
PROBLEM SOLVING

14. Ⓕ Ⓖ Ⓗ Ⓙ Ⓚ
15. Ⓐ Ⓑ Ⓒ Ⓓ Ⓔ
16. Ⓕ Ⓖ Ⓗ Ⓙ Ⓚ
17. Ⓐ Ⓑ Ⓒ Ⓓ Ⓔ
18. Ⓕ Ⓖ Ⓗ Ⓙ Ⓚ
19. Ⓐ Ⓑ Ⓒ Ⓓ Ⓔ
20. Ⓕ Ⓖ Ⓗ Ⓙ Ⓚ
21. Ⓐ Ⓑ Ⓒ Ⓓ Ⓔ
22. Ⓕ Ⓖ Ⓗ Ⓙ Ⓚ
23. Ⓐ Ⓑ Ⓒ Ⓓ Ⓔ
24. Ⓕ Ⓖ Ⓗ Ⓙ Ⓚ
25. Ⓐ Ⓑ Ⓒ Ⓓ Ⓔ
26. Ⓕ Ⓖ Ⓗ Ⓙ Ⓚ

answer sheet

Practice Test 1

PART 1: VERBAL

13 Questions • 20 Minutes

QUESTIONS 1–2: SCRAMBLED PARAGRAPHS

Directions: The paragraph below consists of six sentences in scrambled order. The first, or topic, sentence is given, and you are to arrange the rest in an order that makes sense, each sentence following from the one before in that it explains the earlier one or adds to it.

Write the numbers to the left of the letters (in pencil so you can change them as often as you need). When you are satisfied, mark your choices on the answer sheet.

Because you get no partial credit for having only some of the sentences in a paragraph in order and because trying different arrangements to find which reads best requires more time than other test questions, each of the scrambled paragraphs carries twice the weight of other questions on the test.

1. In media stories about Timothy McVeigh, the convicted and finally executed Oklahoma City bomber, it has been reported that he had not only read but also sold copies of the book called *The Turner Diaries*.

_____**Q.** The book was written in 1978 by Dr. William Pierce, head of a neo-Nazi group called the National Alliance.

_____**R.** While *The Turner Diaries* is sold mostly at gun shows, Dr. Pierce has upped his promotional efforts to bookstores since the Oklahoma bombing.

_____**S.** In it, Pierce tells of a fictional race war in America won, of course, by white supremacists like himself.

_____**T.** That war starts out with the destruction of a federal building by a truck armed with fuel oil and an ammonium nitrate fertilizer bomb like the one used in the Oklahoma City bombing.

_____**U.** By now, there are hundreds of thousands of these dangerous books in circulation, helping to turn malcontents into terrorists.

The second sentence is   Ⓠ Ⓡ Ⓢ Ⓣ Ⓤ
The third sentence is   Ⓠ Ⓡ Ⓢ Ⓣ Ⓤ
The fourth sentence is   Ⓠ Ⓡ Ⓢ Ⓣ Ⓤ
The fifth sentence is   Ⓠ Ⓡ Ⓢ Ⓣ Ⓤ
The sixth sentence is   Ⓠ Ⓡ Ⓢ Ⓣ Ⓤ

2. The human male, hearing for the first time about the heartrending love-life of the male praying mantis, would wonder that the species continues.

_____Q. The anxiety comes from an instinctual awareness that he is likely to quite literally lose his head during mating; this dread seems to slow the process for up to several hours.

_____R. In response, the female who is locked beneath him turns her head and, if she can manage to, bites his head off.

_____S. Though now dead, he remains locked in mating position, and of course the anxiety is ended.

_____T. The release of his sperm speeds up after his demise, assuring a large supply of future praying mantises (who, in the manner of insects, have no further use for the progenitor).

_____U. But in the insect world, romance is not an issue—the drive to reproduce is—so the male praying mantis mounts the much larger female despite his anxiety.

The second sentence is   Ⓠ Ⓡ Ⓢ Ⓣ Ⓤ
The third sentence is   Ⓠ Ⓡ Ⓢ Ⓣ Ⓤ
The fourth sentence is   Ⓠ Ⓡ Ⓢ Ⓣ Ⓤ
The fifth sentence is   Ⓠ Ⓡ Ⓢ Ⓣ Ⓤ
The sixth sentence is   Ⓠ Ⓡ Ⓢ Ⓣ Ⓤ

QUESTIONS 3–5: LOGICAL REASONING

Directions: Read each question very carefully and choose the **best** answer from the five choices given. Select your answer based **only** on the information provided.

3. What five-letter sequence is formed from the word ASTER by replacing the second letter with the fourth, exchanging the first and third, then placing the fifth in the fourth position, and finally placing the remaining letter in the position left open?

A. TARES

B. TASER

C. TESAR

D. TEARS

E. TRAES

4. Bo is taller than Mo, Flo is shorter than Bo, and Ho is taller than Flo but shorter than Mo. So we can deduce that:

F. Bo is shorter than Ho.

G. Mo is shorter than Ho.

H. Flo is taller than Ho.

J. Flo is shorter than Mo.

K. Mo is shorter than Flo.

The problem below uses a code where one specific letter stands for a word and only that word. The letter representing a word usually is not located directly above the word it represents. Each line of letters stands for the words in the line below.

(1) M   X   R   Q   S means

"Jo   drinks   cocoa   and   tea."

(2) V   A   S   W   M means

"Pete   loves   coffee   and   fries."

(3) M   W   Q   U   S means

"Sammy   drinks   coffee   and   cocoa."

(4) M   Z   S   Y   X means

"Sammy   loves   tea   and   cake."

5. Which letter represents the word cake?

A. M

B. Z

C. Y

D. X

E. Cannot be determined from the information given.

QUESTIONS 6–13: READING PASSAGES

Directions: Read each passage below and answer the questions that follow. Remember to **use only the information you have read in the passage** when answering the questions; you may reread the passage if necessary.

Diane Sawyer, the well-known television host, is quick to tell interested young people that making it in television is not as easy as it looks from afar.

5　　She began in journalism working for CBS as a "stakeout," the reporter who spends hours on windy corners waiting to buttonhole reluctant news headliners for an interview. Meanwhile
10　the anchorperson, ensconced in the warm studio, is having his or her hair readied for the camera.

　　Back in her high school days in Louisville, KY, Ms. Sawyer was a cheerleader,
15　and then did a year as Miss American Teenager. During that year, she said, "I traveled on airplanes wearing my crown and scepter. It was awful." Her notoriety that year dampened her social life for
20　four years in college. "People bothered with me at all only so they could say, 'See, she's not so hot.'" Consequently, she studied a good deal and "majored in identity crisis."

25　　Her very first job on television was as a weatherperson in her hometown. "I was so nearsighted, I couldn't tell the western half of the map from the eastern end." Her worst moment was the night
30　she signed off by saying, "Today's high was 71. Temperature right now, 77."

6. Which of the following is the best title for this passage?

　F. Getting Started in Show Business

　G. The Stakeout

　H. How Diane Sawyer Got Her Career Start

　J. Why You Need to Study

　K. The Worst Embarrassment

7. Being Miss American Teenager

　A. was Diane Sawyer's favorite year.

　B. led to Diane Sawyer's anchorperson job.

　C. dampened Diane Sawyer's social life during college.

　D. was just like being a weatherperson.

　E. was all work and no play.

8. The job of a TV reporter

　F. is the same as that of an anchorperson.

　G. is harder and less glamorous than the anchorperson's.

　H. is easy to get.

　J. requires being a weatherperson first.

　K. is a natural consequence of cheerleading.

9. Which of the following does this passage imply?

　A. Diane Sawyer is very conceited.

　B. It's easy for a pretty young woman to be famous on TV.

　C. Diane Sawyer had little formal education.

　D. Diane Sawyer is a down-to-earth, honest woman.

　E. Popularity in school is very important.

Dental treatment has not changed drastically over the years. Cavities are still filled; root canal operations still save decaying teeth; crowns, caps, and bridges
5 replace broken or missing teeth; crooked teeth are still straightened with braces. In fact, about the only widely used new treatments are implants for false teeth and bonding for ugly ones. And they don't
10 always work.

But, although treatments themselves have changed little, the techniques, tools, and materials that dentists use are constantly being upgraded.

15 The old chair which the dentist used to pump into position with a foot pedal is gone, replaced by one that glides silently into position at the push of a button, often permitting the patient to recline at the
20 dentist's work level.

Replacing drill handles scattered overhead, their belts and pulleys in frightening view, is a compact arrangement of "handpieces" convenient to the dentist's
25 reach. All motor parts are condensed and concealed.

In place of the blinding searchlight, which used to be trained on your open mouth, is a probing mirror with its own
30 high-intensity light. And the overhead beam is confined to your mouth area.

That old torture instrument, the drill, no longer must be pressed down forcibly, or stopped periodically while
35 it cools off (thus adding to the suspense of the torture). Today it is a high-speed, water-cooled device. It can, however, still hurt when a nerve is struck.

It is unlikely that in the foreseeable
40 future a trip to the dentist will be an eagerly anticipated treat, but at least it should take less time and give better results.

10. Which of the following best describes the theme of this passage?

   F. Dentistry through the years.

   G. Dental treatment has changed little with the times, but the equipment used keeps improving.

   H. Dental implants and bonding have revolutionized dentistry.

J. Dentistry will soon be painless as equipment and technology progress.

K. In the field of dentistry, nothing ever changes, with the exception of dentists themselves.

11. Positioning the patient for dental treatment today

   A. involves new mirrors, allowing varied reclined positions.

   B. no longer involves belts and pulleys to move up or down.

   C. involves a pedal glider easily accessible to the dentist.

   D. involves new treatments and new machinery activated by switches.

   E. is done at the push of a button, producing smooth movements.

12. In the old days, drilling was one of the most feared parts of dental treatment because

   F. the drill could go through the nerve and cause severe bleeding and pain.

   G. it was too loud, too painful, and too costly.

   H. sometimes the wrong tooth was drilled, causing unnecessary suffering.

   J. it never cured the cavity and the pain was excessive.

   K. the dentist pushed down with the instrument and had to stop constantly to let the drill cool.

13. A dentist's handpiece today is

   A. attached to pulleys that are small and nonfrightening.

   B. the scary part, because of its threatening shape.

   C. like a wrench in shape and function.

   D. compact, with its working parts hidden.

   E. used instead of a pulley for manual work.

PART II: MATHEMATICS
13 Questions • 20 Minutes

The following information is provided for your reference. It will likely not appear in the actual test booklet. You should memorize these formulas and symbols.

FORMULAS

- Area of a circle (with radius r) = πr^2

- Circumference of a circle = $2\pi r$

- Area of a parallelogram (with base b and height h) = bh

- Area of a trapezoid (with parallel sides a and b and height h) = $\frac{1}{2}(a+b)h$

- Volume of a cone or pyramid (with base area b and height h) = $\frac{1}{3}bh$

- Volume of a cylinder (with base area b and height h) = bh

- Volume of a sphere $\left(\text{with radius } r\right)$ = $\frac{4}{3}\pi r^3$

- Sum of the measures of the angles of a triangle = $180°$

- Area of a triangle:

$$\text{Area} = \frac{bh}{2}$$

- For a right triangle:

$$c^2 = a^2 + b^2$$

DEFINITIONS OF SYMBOLS

=   is equal to

≠   is unequal to

<   is less than

>   is greater than

≤   is less than or equal to

≥   is greater than or equal to

⊥   is perpendicular to

∥   is parallel to

∠   angle

└   right angle

⇉ parallel lines

NOTES

- Figures may not be drawn to scale. Do not assume any relationship in a diagram unless it is specifically stated or can be figured out from given information.

- Assume that a diagram is in one plane unless the problem specifically states that it is not.

- Reduce all fractions to lowest terms.

QUESTIONS 14–26: PROBLEM SOLVING

Directions: For each question, solve the problem and select the best answer from the choices given.

14. $15^2 + (-3)^3 - 1^2 =$

   F. 11^3

   G. 251

   H. 11^7

   J. 197

   K. 30

15. Solve for x: $x + 2 = \dfrac{5}{3x}$

   A. 3

   B. 0.75

   C. – 3

   D. 2

   E. 1.25

16. What is the length of side x of the triangle shown below?

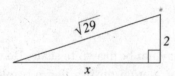

   F. $\sqrt{5}$

   G. 25

   H. $\sqrt{33}$

   J. 5

   K. $\sqrt{31}$

17. $\left[(-2)(4) - (2)(-1)\right] \div \dfrac{1}{2} =$

   A. 1

   B. 12

   C. –3

   D. –12

   E. 20

18. $4.23 + 60.0 + 0.354 =$

   F. 837

   G. 64.584

   H. 10.584

   J. 5.184

   K. 13.77

19. Sammy pitched eight games and won five of them. To the nearest percent, what percent of games did Sammy lose?

   A. 50%

   B. 30%

   C. 40%

   D. 63%

   E. 38%

20. Which of the following shows an isosceles triangle?

   F.

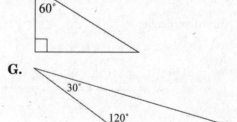

   G.

   H.

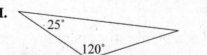

   J.

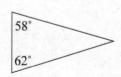

   K.

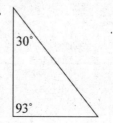

21. Carol bought a coat for $60.00. This was 75% of its original price. By how much was the coat reduced?

   A. $80.00

   B. $45.00

   C. $40.00

   D. $50.00

   E. $20.00

22. In the figure shown, each segment is 10 centimeters long, and all angles are right angles. The area of the shaded region is

   F. 150 cm²

   G. 200 cm²

   H. 225 cm²

   J. 175 cm²

   K. None of these

23. What is $\frac{1}{4}\%$ of 2800?

   A. 700

   B. 0.07

   C. 7

   D. 0.7

   E. 70

24.

```
   A   B   C   D   E   F   G   H   I   J
 <-|---|---|---|---|---|---|---|---|---|--->
  -8  -6  -4  -2   0   2   4   6   8  10
```

The sum of the coordinates of which points on the number line above would be equal to zero?

   F. B, D, E, I

   G. C, D, G, H

   H. A, C, F, I

   J. D, E, F, G

   K. B, C, H, I

25. How many fourths are there in $\frac{5}{6}$?

   A. $\frac{5}{24}$

   B. $\frac{7}{12}$

   C. $1\frac{1}{2}$

   D. 2

   E. $3\frac{1}{3}$

26. The average of –10, 6, 0, –3, and 22 is

   F. 4

   G. 3

   H. 2

   J. –3

   K. –6

ANSWER KEY AND EXPLANATIONS

1. QSTRU	7. C	12. K	17. D	22. G
2. UQRST	8. G	13. D	18. G	23. C
3. D	9. D	14. J	19. E	24. F
4. J	10. G	15. A	20. G	25. E
5. E	11. E	16. J	21. E	26. G
6. H				

PART I: VERBAL
SCRAMBLED PARAGRAPHS

1. **The correct order is QSTRU.** Q is the second sentence because it gives the name and author of the book in the topic sentence. S is third because it tells something about the book that relates to the topic sentence. T is fourth because it starts with "that war," denoting the war mentioned in the second sentence. R is fifth because it returns to the topic and could not follow the sixth sentence but must precede it. U is sixth because it smoothly connects with the fifth sentence and concludes the topic idea.

2. **The correct order is UQRST.** U is the second sentence because it continues the explanation of the praying mantis's love-life in human terms. Q is third because it continues the thought of the anxiety in the preceding sentence. R is fourth because it continues from the second sentence to an explanation. S is fifth because it continues the action. T is sixth because it concludes the action.

LOGICAL REASONING

3. **The correct answer is D.** Write the word and carry out each step carefully (see below):

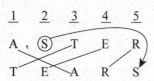

4. **The correct answer is J.** Set up a ladder and enter each person in order by height (see below). By checking each answer choice next to diagram 3, the only correct one is answer J.

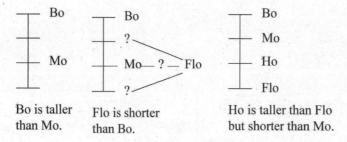

Bo is taller than Mo.

Flo is shorter than Bo.

Ho is taller than Flo but shorter than Mo.

5. **The correct answer is E.** *Cake* has to be one of the five letters in the last sentence, M, Z, S, Y, and X. *Cake* is present only in sentence 4, therefore, eliminate any of the letters in sentence 4 present in the other three sentences M̶, Z, S̶, Y, X̶. This leaves Z and Y, so you don't have enough information. The correct answer is E. You would have arrived at the same answer if you checked through the sentence 4 words and found that *Jen* and *cake* only appear in sentence 4. You could not know which of the two letters appearing only in sentence 4 coded for *Jen* and which coded for *cake*.

NOTE: All the code problems involve finding common letters and words in the four sentences. In this way, words and their codes can be found. As an example, look at the four sentences, each has the word "and" in the sentence. Look at the letters over each sentence to find what letter or letters appear in every line. Only "M" appears in all four sentences, therefore "M" must stand for *and*.

READING PASSAGES

6. **The correct answer is H.** Choice F is wrong because the passage is not about how a person should start out in show business, nor is it about show business in general. Choices G and K are wrong because they are each just mentioned briefly and neither is the subject of the passage. Choice J is not mentioned. Choice H is the subject of this passage.

7. **The correct answer is C.** The passage offers no support for choices A, B, D, or E. But the third paragraph states that being Miss American Teenager "dampened her social life for four years in college."

8. **The correct answer is G.** Choice G is supported by the second paragraph, which contrasts the job of the reporter who spends hours on a cold windy corner and the anchorperson ensconced in the warm studio having his or her hair readied for the camera.

9. **The correct answer is D.** Choice A is wrong: she seems quite the opposite, and the passage brings out that it was not easy to get where she did. Choice C is wrong because the passage says she went to college, and choice E is wrong because the passage indicates the opposite. Choice D is correct because that is what comes through in what she says.

10. **The correct answer is G.** The passage is all about what's new and what's old in dentistry. The new equipment is discussed at length. Choice F is too general. Choices H and J are misstatements. Choice K is wrong.

11. **The correct answer is E.** The third paragraph states that all the new chairs glide into position with the push of a button. Choices A, B, C, and D are wrong because each contains something incorrect.

12. **The correct answer is K.** The next-to-last paragraph says it all. The old drill got hot and had to be pressed into the tooth. Choice F mentions nerve pain, but you can reject it as it doesn't follow from the passage. Choices G, H, and J are riddled with statements totally outside the passage's content.

13. **The correct answer is D.** The fourth paragraph discusses the new "handpieces" with their small and hidden working parts. Choice A is wrong because pulleys are not modern; choices B, C, and E are not mentioned in the passage.

Part II: Mathematics

PROBLEM SOLVING

14. The correct answer is J.

$$15^2 + (-3)^3 - 1^2 = (15)(15) + (-3)(-3)(-3) - (1)(1)$$
$$= 225 + (-27) - 1$$
$$= 197$$

15. The correct answer is A.

$$x + 2 = \frac{5}{3}x$$
$$2 = \frac{5}{3}x - x$$
$$2 = \frac{5}{3}x - \frac{3}{3}x$$
$$2 = \frac{2}{3}x$$
$$1 = \frac{1}{3}x$$
$$3 = x$$

16. The correct answer is J. Using the Pythagorean theorem, $a^2 + b^2 = c^2$, and substituting

$$2^2 + x^2 = \left(\sqrt{29}\right)^2, \text{ we get}$$

$$4 + x^2 = 29$$
$$-4 = -4$$
$$x^2 = 25$$
$$x = \sqrt{25}; \text{ therefore } x = 5$$

17. The correct answer is D.

$$\left[(-2)(4) - (2)(-1)\right] \div \frac{1}{2} = \left[-8 - (-2)\right] \div \frac{1}{2} = [-6] \div \frac{1}{2}$$
$$= -6 \times 2$$
$$= -12$$

18. The correct answer is G. Add:

```
  4.23
 60.0
  .354
64.584
```

19. The correct answer is E. 5 out of 8 is the ratio of games won to games played. Therefore, 3 out of 8 is the ratio of games lost to total games played.

$$\frac{3}{8} \text{ as a decimal} = 3 \div 8 = 8 \overline{)3.00}^{\,0.37\frac{1}{2}}$$

$0.37\frac{1}{2}$ as a percent is $37\frac{1}{2}\%$. The nearest percent is 38%.

20. **The correct answer is G.** Find the third angle in each triangle; remember, the sum of the measures of the angles in a triangle is 180°. The triangle with two equal angles is isosceles.

F.

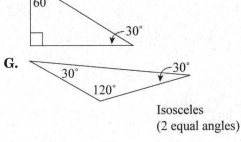

G.

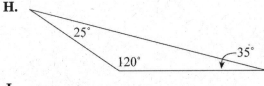

Isosceles
(2 equal angles)

H.

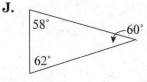

J.

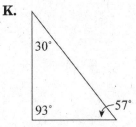

K.

21. **The correct answer is E.** $60 = 75\%$ of the original price, or $60 = 0.75 \times$ original price. To find the original price, divide by 0.75:

$$.75\overline{)60.00} = 80$$

$$\begin{array}{r} 80 \\ .75\overline{)60.00} \\ \underline{60\ 0} \\ 0 \end{array}$$

$80 - $60 = 20

22. **The correct answer is G.** Since the area of a equals the area of b, the shaded area is really the area of two squares with 10 cm sides: $10^2 + 10^2 = 200$ cm².

23. The correct answer is C. $\frac{1}{4}\%$ of 2800 means $0.25\% \times 2800$, or 0.0025×2800, which equals:

$$
\begin{array}{r}
2800 \\
\times\ \ .0025 \\
\hline
14000 \\
56000 \\
\hline
7.0000
\end{array}
$$

24. The correct answer is F. $-6 + -2 + 0 + 8 = 0$

25. The correct answer is E. Simply divide $\frac{5}{6}$ by $\frac{1}{4}$.

$$
\begin{aligned}
\frac{5}{6} \div \frac{1}{4} &= \frac{5}{6} \cdot \frac{4}{1} \\
&= \frac{20}{6} \\
&= 3\frac{1}{3}
\end{aligned}
$$

26. The correct answer is G. To find the average, find the sum of the addends and divide that sum by the number of addends.

$$
-10 + 6 + 0 + -3 + 22 = 15
$$
$$
15 \div 5 = 3
$$

ANSWER SHEET PRACTICE TEST 2
Part I: Verbal

Scrambled Paragraphs

Paragraph 1

The second sentence is Ⓠ Ⓡ Ⓢ Ⓣ Ⓤ

The third sentence is Ⓠ Ⓡ Ⓢ Ⓣ Ⓤ

The fourth sentence is Ⓠ Ⓡ Ⓢ Ⓣ Ⓤ

The fifth sentence is Ⓠ Ⓡ Ⓢ Ⓣ Ⓤ

The sixth sentence is Ⓠ Ⓡ Ⓢ Ⓣ Ⓤ

Paragraph 2

The second sentence is Ⓠ Ⓡ Ⓢ Ⓣ Ⓤ

The third sentence is Ⓠ Ⓡ Ⓢ Ⓣ Ⓤ

The fourth sentence is Ⓠ Ⓡ Ⓢ Ⓣ Ⓤ

The fifth sentence is Ⓠ Ⓡ Ⓢ Ⓣ Ⓤ

The sixth sentence is Ⓠ Ⓡ Ⓢ Ⓣ Ⓤ

Logical Reasoning

3. Ⓐ Ⓑ Ⓒ Ⓓ Ⓔ

4. Ⓕ Ⓖ Ⓗ Ⓙ Ⓚ

5. Ⓐ Ⓑ Ⓒ Ⓓ Ⓔ

Reading

6. Ⓕ Ⓖ Ⓗ Ⓙ Ⓚ

7. Ⓐ Ⓑ Ⓒ Ⓓ Ⓔ

8. Ⓕ Ⓖ Ⓗ Ⓙ Ⓚ

9. Ⓐ Ⓑ Ⓒ Ⓓ Ⓔ

10. Ⓕ Ⓖ Ⓗ Ⓙ Ⓚ

11. Ⓐ Ⓑ Ⓒ Ⓓ Ⓔ

12. Ⓕ Ⓖ Ⓗ Ⓙ Ⓚ

13. Ⓐ Ⓑ Ⓒ Ⓓ Ⓔ

PART II: MATHEMATICS
PROBLEM SOLVING

14. Ⓕ Ⓖ Ⓗ Ⓙ Ⓚ

15. Ⓐ Ⓑ Ⓒ Ⓓ Ⓔ

16. Ⓕ Ⓖ Ⓗ Ⓙ Ⓚ

17. Ⓐ Ⓑ Ⓒ Ⓓ Ⓔ

18. Ⓕ Ⓖ Ⓗ Ⓙ Ⓚ

19. Ⓐ Ⓑ Ⓒ Ⓓ Ⓔ

20. Ⓕ Ⓖ Ⓗ Ⓙ Ⓚ

21. Ⓐ Ⓑ Ⓒ Ⓓ Ⓔ

22. Ⓕ Ⓖ Ⓗ Ⓙ Ⓚ

23. Ⓐ Ⓑ Ⓒ Ⓓ Ⓔ

24. Ⓕ Ⓖ Ⓗ Ⓙ Ⓚ

25. Ⓐ Ⓑ Ⓒ Ⓓ Ⓔ

26. Ⓕ Ⓖ Ⓗ Ⓙ Ⓚ

answer sheet

Practice Test 2

PART 1: VERBAL

13 Questions • 20 Minutes
QUESTIONS 1–2: SCRAMBLED PARAGRAPHS

Directions: The paragraph below consists of six sentences in scrambled order. The first, or topic, sentence is given, and you are to arrange the rest in an order that makes sense, each sentence following from the one before in that it explains the earlier one or adds to it.

Write the numbers to the left of the letters (in pencil so you can change them as often as you need). When you are satisfied, mark your choices on the answer sheet.

Because you get no partial credit for having only some of the sentences in a paragraph in order and because trying different arrangements to find which reads best requires more time than other test questions, each of the scrambled paragraphs carries twice the weight of other questions on the test.

1. From Lenin on, Communist leaders recognized the importance of mind control as the way to force reluctant people to do their bidding.

   _____**Q.** One of these techniques, especially favored by North Korean prisoner-of-war camp guards, was to torture the prisoner through starvation, sleep deprivation, and cruel beatings until he was near death.

   _____**R.** This same kind of brainwashing was used to torture Americans captured during the Vietnam War, the most prominent of whom was the courageous Senator John McCain.

   _____**S.** Then they would "save him," only to repeat the entire process.

   _____**T.** The subtle psychological techniques employed to break political or war prisoners and extract information or obedience from them was known as brainwashing.

   _____**U.** Eventually, the prisoner would be so grateful to his captors for saving him from death so often, he would be almost happy to do whatever they wanted.

   The second sentence is Ⓠ Ⓡ Ⓢ Ⓣ Ⓤ
   The third sentence is   Ⓠ Ⓡ Ⓢ Ⓣ Ⓤ
   The fourth sentence is Ⓠ Ⓡ Ⓢ Ⓣ Ⓤ
   The fifth sentence is   Ⓠ Ⓡ Ⓢ Ⓣ Ⓤ
   The sixth sentence is   Ⓠ Ⓡ Ⓢ Ⓣ Ⓤ

2. Have you ever wondered what kind of work you might be doing if you decided on a career in physics and successfully completed your education in that field?

_____**Q.** Physicists who are experts at bodies in rest or motion contribute to the building of bridges, roads, even vehicles, while those who specialize in thermodynamics are needed to design engines and refrigerators.

_____**R.** Physicists in still other areas of the sciences design a nearly endless list of other human needs, among them telescopes, nuclear plants, and medical equipment.

_____**S.** Many industries employ physicists to find ways to improve manufacturing processes or products.

_____**T.** Another area of specialization is sound: the design of such diverse products as auditoriums, hearing aids, and recording equipment.

_____**U.** You could do research in a commercial laboratory or in a university, testing physical theories with practical applications.

The second sentence is   Ⓠ Ⓡ Ⓢ Ⓣ Ⓤ

The third sentence is   Ⓠ Ⓡ Ⓢ Ⓣ Ⓤ

The fourth sentence is   Ⓠ Ⓡ Ⓢ Ⓣ Ⓤ

The fifth sentence is   Ⓠ Ⓡ Ⓢ Ⓣ Ⓤ

The sixth sentence is   Ⓠ Ⓡ Ⓢ Ⓣ Ⓤ

QUESTIONS 3–5: LOGICAL REASONING

Directions: Read each question very carefully and choose the **best** answer from the five choices given. Select your answer based **only** on the information provided.

3. Which letter in the name CAMERON is two letters before the third letter preceding the last letter?

   A. C

   B. A

   C. M

   D. E

   E. R

4. Tawana, Ida, Sonia, Amy, and Rita are friends. Ida is shorter than more than half of her friends. Rita is shorter than all but one of the girls. Sonia is separated from Amy by one girl. Amy is taller than Tawana. Going from the tallest to shortest, what is their order of height?

   F. Sonia, Amy, Tawana, Ida, Rita

   G. Amy, Tawana, Sonia, Rita, Ida

   H. Tawana, Amy, Ida, Rita, Sonia

   J. Amy, Rita, Tawana, Sonia, Ida

   K. Sonia, Tawana, Amy, Ida, Rita

The problem below uses a code where one specific letter stands for a word and only that word. The letters are scrambled and NEVER placed above the word it represents. Each line of letters stands for the words in the lines below.

(1) M   X   R   Q   S   means

Jackie   drinks   cocoa   and   tea.

(2) V   L   S   W   O   means

Pedro   loves   coffee   and   fries.

(3) M   W   Q   U   S   means

Barach   drinks   coffee   and   cocoa.

(4) O   Z   S   Y   X   means

Jema   loves   tea   and   cake.

5. Which word is represented by the letter V?

   A. Pedro

   B. loves

   C. coffee

   D. and

   E. fries

QUESTIONS 6–13: READING PASSAGES

Directions: Read each passage below and answer the questions that follow. Remember to **use only the information you have read in the passage** when answering the questions; you may reread the passage if necessary.

Gasoline prices at the pump vary from station to station by as much as 30 cents a gallon for the same gas. Have you ever wondered why?

5   The price of gas is set by the retailer. Gas station owners operate in a free market. The price they charge depends upon many factors: the amount of gas each sells weekly, competition from

10 nearby stations, the profit margin the owner seeks, whether the station makes most of its money in its service bays or from pumping gas, the rent and other overhead paid in that area, how liberal

15 a charge policy the station maintains, the amount of service offered the gas customer, the "tank-wagon price" paid to the distributor (which may depend on the retailer's volume), and, finally, what

20 the market will bear.

On a busy highway, or in a dense commercial center, where gas stations are cheek by jowl with one another, competition keeps prices down. These

25 stations need to sell gas because most of their customers are just driving through and will not bring their cars in for service.

The small-town gas station, with little competition, sells relatively little

30 gas, for which it pays a higher price, and renders more service. The overhead may or may not be higher than that of the urban station, but you can be pretty sure to pay more for your gas there.

6. Which of the following best tells what this passage is about?

F. Free-market dollars in the oil business

G. Problems of the automobile owner

H. Why gas prices are different at different stations

J. How gasoline is taxed

K. Satisfying the gasoline customer

7. According to this passage, retail gas prices are influenced by

A. seasons.

B. sales quotas.

C. organized crime.

D. location.

E. whimsy.

8. Gas stations in areas where gas stations are few

F. drive up gas prices in busy intersections.

G. charge less for gas.

H. don't service cars.

J. tend to charge more for gas.

K. sell more gas.

9. The price you pay for gas

A. depends on the individual station owner.

B. involves the distributor.

C varies with volume sold.

D. is lower where there is not much auto servicing.

E. All of the above

Aristotle, the great philosopher who lived and thought about religion, humanity, and art roughly three hundred years before Christ, was also

5   well known in his time as a scientist. The great minds of his time gave their attention to everything because the available knowledge was not so vast and so diversified as it is now. But while

10 Aristotle's writings on literature and philosophy are still standard reading, his scientific discoveries have been

refined or disproved by the many great scientists who have followed.

15   One of the scientific ideas that engaged Aristotle, though he didn't have the name for it, was the concept of gravity. Through simple experimentation and complicated analysis, he came to
20 the conclusion that heavier objects fell to the earth from above faster than lighter ones. Dropping a stone and a feather simultaneously, and observing that the stone landed first, he attributed
25 the stone's greater speed of descent to its extra weight and the fact that it was made of earth. The natural motion of an object composed of earth, he wrongly supposed, was toward the center of the
30 earth, while objects such as the feather would not have this tendency.

    Pursuing his findings further, Aristotle came upon the notion of physical resistance. He realized that wind would
35 offer more resistance to the fall of the light feather than to the rock. We have long known (and you could prove it yourself) that a stone and a feather dropped together inside a vacuum would land at
40 exactly the same instant because without the air there would be no resistance to either object, and the law of gravity would prevail.

    Aristotle never came up with the
45 mathematical formula later discovered to govern the speed of falling bodies, which is an outcome of the law of gravity, but for hundreds of years scientists didn't care. Aristotle's theory fit ordinary experience
50 well enough. And after all, the study of the motion of objects in space interested only a few scholars. So for hundreds of years, Aristotle's theories stood.

10. What is this passage chiefly about?

F. The way of falling bodies

G. Gravity from ancient times to now

H. Aristotle's contribution to understanding gravity

J. Why Aristotle's philosophy made him famous

K. What causes gravity

11. According to the passage, Aristotle believed that

A. falling bodies were not equally influenced by wind.

B. resistance to gravity is mathematically explainable.

C. others would carry his work forward.

D. the earth attracted all things equally.

E. his experiments dealt with something called gravity.

12. Which of the following can be inferred from what is written in the passage?

F. The earth's air somehow influences the speed of falling bodies.

G. Scientists of the day scoffed at Aristotle's scientific theories.

H. Astronomy was to provide the key to further understanding of the law of gravity.

J. Aristotle thought water would fall slower than a rock.

K. The existence of a stopwatch would have enabled Aristotle to work out the math.

13. Which of the following represents one premise on which Aristotle based his theories that was false?

A. Physical resistance influences falling bodies.

B. Objects made of earth exclusively head for earth's center.

C. One pound of feathers weighs less than one pound of rocks.

D. The earth is the center of the universe.

E. There is no mathematical way to portray the speed of falling bodies.

PART II: MATHEMATICS

13 Questions • 20 Minutes

The following information is provided for your reference. It will likely not appear in the actual test booklet. You should memorize these formulas and symbols.

FORMULAS

- Area of a circle (with radius r) $= \pi r^2$

- Circumference of a circle $= 2\pi r$

- Area of a parallelogram (with base b and height h) $= bh$

- Area of a trapezoid (with parallel sides a and b and height h) $= \frac{1}{2}(a+b)h$

- Volume of a cone or pyramid (with base area b and height h) $= \frac{1}{3}bh$

- Volume of a cylinder (with base area b and height h) $= bh$

- Volume of a sphere $\left(\text{with radius } r\right) = \frac{4}{3}\pi r^3$

- Sum of the measures of the angles of a triangle $= 180°$

- Area of a triangle:

$$\text{Area} = \frac{bh}{2}$$

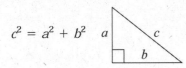

- For a right triangle:

$$c^2 = a^2 + b^2$$

DEFINITIONS OF SYMBOLS

$=$ is equal to

$\neq$ is unequal to

$<$ is less than

$>$ is greater than

$\leq$ is less than or equal to

$\geq$ is greater than or equal to

$\perp$ is perpendicular to

$\parallel$ is parallel to

$\angle$ angle

$\llcorner$ right angle

$\rightrightarrows$ parallel lines

NOTES

- Figures may not be drawn to scale. Do not assume any relationship in a diagram unless it is specifically stated or can be figured out from given information.

- Assume that a diagram is in one plane unless the problem specifically states that it is not.

- Reduce all fractions to lowest terms.

QUESTIONS 14–26: PROBLEM SOLVING

Directions: For each question, solve the problem and select the best answer from the choices given.

14. If $0.05x = 1.5$, then $2x =$

    F. 30

    G. 0.075

    H. 15

    J. 60

    K. 6.0

15. The volume of a rectangular solid whose length is 15 inches, height is 10 inches, and width is 5 inches, is

    A. 800 in.³

    B. 7.5 in.³

    C. 75 in.³

    D. 10 ft.³

    E. 750 in.³

16. 175% of 80 is

    F. 1.4

    G. 14,000

    H. 140

    J. 14

    K. 1400

17. When $\dfrac{a^5}{2}$ is divided by $3a^2$, the quotient is

    A. $6a^7$

    B. $\dfrac{2}{3}a^{\frac{5}{2}}$

    C. $1\dfrac{1}{2}$

    D. $\dfrac{a^3}{6}$

    E. $\dfrac{3}{2}a^{\frac{2}{5}}$

18. If x gallons of paint cost 8y dollars, what is the cost in dollars of $1\dfrac{1}{2}$ gallons of paint?

    F. 16xy

    G. $\dfrac{8y}{3x}$

    H. $\dfrac{3x}{2y}$

    J. $\dfrac{3}{2}xy$

    K. $\dfrac{12y}{x}$

19. If $4x = 10$ and $2y = 4x$, then $y =$

    A. 5

    B. $2\dfrac{1}{2}$

    C 10

    D. $\dfrac{1}{2}$

    E. 4

20. The square root of 6.25 is

    F. 0.025

    G. 0.25

    H. 2.5

    J. 25

    K. 312

21. $\dfrac{x^2}{x^5} \times \dfrac{x^{12}}{x^9}$

    A. x

    B. $\dfrac{1}{x}$

    C. 1

    D. x^{14}

    E. None of these

22. If the area of the base of a circular pool is 300 square yards, what is its radius? (Area of a circle is: $A = \pi r^2$; $\pi = 3.14$)

  F. Less than 10 yards

  G. More than 25 yards

  H. Between 10 and 15 yards

  J. 20 yards

  K. None of these

23.

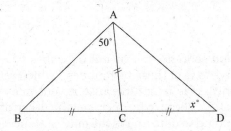

If AC = BC = DC, then x =

  A. 40

  B. 50

  C. 45

  D. 30

  E. 35

24. How much larger than 80 is 100?

  F. 18%

  G. 20%

  H. 25%

  J. 35%

  K. 40%

25. If $\frac{3}{8}$" on a scale drawing is equivalent to one foot at full scale, what distance on the drawing will stand for forty inches?

  A. $\frac{1}{8}$ inch

  B. $\frac{7}{8}$ inch

  C. $1\frac{1}{4}$ inches

  D. $2\frac{1}{3}$ inches

  E. $8\frac{8}{9}$ inches

26. $6 \div \frac{1}{3} + \frac{2}{3} \times 9 =$

  F. $\frac{2}{3}$

  G. 11

  H. 24

  J. 54

  K. 168

ANSWER KEY AND EXPLANATIONS

1. TQSUR	7. D	12. H	17. D	22. F
2. USQTR	8. J	13. B	18. K	23. A
3. B	9. E	14. J	19. A	24. H
4. G	10. H	15. E	20. H	25. C
5. E	11. A	16. H	21. C	26. H
6. H				

PART I: VERBAL
SCRAMBLED PARAGRAPHS

1. **The correct order is TQSUR.** T is the second sentence because it describes what is meant by mind control. Q is third because it says "one of these techniques," which refers to techniques mentioned in the second sentence. S is fourth because it continues the technique described in the third sentence. U is fifth because it concludes the description above. R is sixth because it brings the paragraph up to date and is the only sentence left.

2. **The correct order is USQTR.** U is the second sentence because it is in answer to the "you" in the topic sentence. S is third because it mentions other roles for general physicists. Q is fourth because it starts a discussion of specialized work. T is fifth because it starts with "another area of specialization," other than that in the fourth sentence. R is sixth because it starts with still other areas, so it must come after the others.

LOGICAL REASONING

3. **The correct answer is B.** Find the third letter before the last letter (see below). Now find the letter that is two letters before that letter.

C A M E R O N
 2 1 3 2 1

4. **The correct answer is G.** (1) Put down the girls' names, placing Ida on the short end of the group. (2) The third sentence tells you that Rita is taller than Ida, so change Rita and Ida. (3) Next, separate Sonia and Amy by one girl, so that Tawana is between them. (4) Finally, you are told that Amy is taller than Tawana, so reverse the order of the three tall girls to find the answer to the question.

Tallest

1) Tawana	2) T	3) S	4) A
Sonia	S	T	T
Amy	A	A	S
Ida	R	R	R
Rita	I	I	I

Shortest

5. **The correct answer is E.** The letter V appears only in sentence 2. Find those words that only appear in sentence 2 and underline them. <u>Pedro</u> loves coffee and <u>fries</u>. Now find the letters that only appear in sentence 2. They are V and L. *Pedro* appears under the letter V and the instructions say a letter is never placed above the word it represents. So V can't stand for Pedro, that leaves *fries* as the only choice for V to represent.

READING PASSAGES

6. **The correct answer is H.** Choice F is meaningless. Choice G is wrong because the only problem of the car owner dealt with in the passage is how not to pay top dollar for gas. Choice K, satisfying the gas customer, is not even mentioned, nor is the gas tax, choice J. Choice H is the correct answer.

7. **The correct answer is D.** All these answers are possibilities, but the only one mentioned in the passage is choice D, location of the station.

8. **The correct answer is J.** Choice F is wrong because there is no connection between prices in different areas. Choices G and H are the opposite of the case, and choice K is never mentioned. Choice J is what the passage says.

9. **The correct answer is E.** Choices A, B, C, and D are all mentioned as factors in the sales price charged for gas.

10. **The correct answer is H.** The passage is all about Aristotle and his work with the concept of gravity. Choices F and G are only touched upon, and choices J and K are not even discussed.

11. **The correct answer is A.** As stated in the third paragraph, Aristotle used wind to partially explain the variance in the falling speed of objects. Choices B, D, and E are actually misstated from the passage, and choice C is not mentioned.

12. **The correct answer is H.** The last paragraph states that Aristotle's theories on falling bodies stood for hundreds of years, and then goes on to imply that the study of the motions of bodies in space would be its undoing. Choice F is flatly stated in the passage. Choices G, J, and K are nowhere mentioned or inferred.

13. **The correct answer is B.** Aristotle believed that objects made of earth had a special attraction to the center of the earth. The passage states at the end of paragraph two that this was wrong. Choice A is true, choices C and D are not mentioned, and choice E is not a false premise of Aristotle.

Part II: Mathematics

PROBLEM SOLVING

14. The correct answer is J.

$$0.05x = 1.5$$
$$5x = 150 \quad \text{(multiply both sides by 100)}$$
$$\frac{5x}{5} = \frac{150}{5} \quad \text{(divide both sides by 5)}$$
$$x = 30$$

Therefore, $2x = 2 \times 30 = 60$

15. The correct answer is E. The volume of a rectangular solid is $V = l \times w \times h$; therefore;

$$V = 15 \times 5 \times 10$$
$$V = 750 \text{ in.}^3$$

16. The correct answer is H. $175\% = 1.75$ as a decimal or $1\frac{3}{4}$ as a fraction; therefore, 175% of $80 =$

$$1.75 \times 80 = 140 \left(\text{or } \frac{7}{\cancel{4}} \times \frac{\cancel{80}^{20}}{1} = 140 \right)$$

17. The correct answer is D. $\dfrac{a^5}{2} \div 3a^2 = \dfrac{a^5}{2} \times \dfrac{1}{3a^2} = \dfrac{a^5}{6a^2} = \dfrac{a^3}{6}$

$$\left(\text{remember:} = \frac{a^5}{a^2} = a^{5-2} = a^3 \right)$$

18. The correct answer is K. If x gallons costs $8y$ dollars,

then 1 gallon costs $\dfrac{8y}{x}$ dollars

and $1\frac{1}{2}$ gallons $= \dfrac{3}{2}$ gallons cost $\dfrac{3}{2} \times \dfrac{8y}{x}$ dollars $= \dfrac{24y}{2x}$ dollars $= \dfrac{12y}{x}$ dollars

19. The correct answer is A. If $4x = 10$ and $4x = 2y$, then $2y = 10$

Dividing both sides by 2: $\dfrac{2y}{2} = \dfrac{10}{2}; y = \dfrac{10}{2}; y = 5$

20. The correct answer is H. The square root of 6.25 is 2.5, since $2.5 \times 2.5 = 6.25$

21. The correct answer is C.

$$\frac{x^2}{x^5} \times \frac{x^{12}}{x^9} = \frac{x^2 \times x^{12}}{x^5 \times x^9} = \frac{x^{2+12}}{x^{5+9}} = \frac{x^{14}}{x^{14}} = 1$$

22. The correct answer is F. If the radius were exactly 10, then the area would be

$A = \pi r^2$
$= 3.14 \times 10 \times 10$
$= 314$

But 314 is greater than 300; therefore, $r < 10$.

23. The correct answer is A. In a triangle, if two sides are equal, then the angles opposite these sides have the same measure.

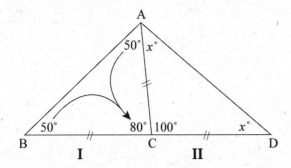

In ∆I, the angles are 50°, 50°, 80°; thus, in ∆II, the angles are $x°$, $x°$, 100°. So,

$x + x + 100° = 180$
$2x = 80$
$x = 40$

24. The correct answer is H. 100 is 20 larger than 80. 20 is one fourth, or 25%, of 80. Therefore, 125% of 80 is equivalent to 100.

25. The correct answer is C. Forty inches equal $3\frac{1}{3}$ feet. Since $\frac{3}{8}''$ equals 1 foot,

$$3\frac{1}{3}\text{ feet} = 3\frac{1}{3} \cdot \frac{3}{8}$$
$$= \frac{10}{3} \cdot \frac{3}{8}$$
$$= \frac{10}{8}$$
$$= 1\frac{1}{4}''$$

26. The correct answer is H. Bracket the multiplication and division first, and solve the problem.

$$\left(6 \div \frac{1}{3}\right) + \left(\frac{2}{3} \times 9\right) = 18 + 6 = 24$$

ANSWER SHEET PRACTICE TEST 3
Part I: Verbal

Scrambled Paragraphs

Paragraph 1

The second sentence is   Ⓠ Ⓡ Ⓢ Ⓣ Ⓤ

The third sentence is   Ⓠ Ⓡ Ⓢ Ⓣ Ⓤ

The fourth sentence is   Ⓠ Ⓡ Ⓢ Ⓣ Ⓤ

The fifth sentence is   Ⓠ Ⓡ Ⓢ Ⓣ Ⓤ

The sixth sentence is   Ⓠ Ⓡ Ⓢ Ⓣ Ⓤ

Paragraph 2

The second sentence is   Ⓠ Ⓡ Ⓢ Ⓣ Ⓤ

The third sentence is   Ⓠ Ⓡ Ⓢ Ⓣ Ⓤ

The fourth sentence is   Ⓠ Ⓡ Ⓢ Ⓣ Ⓤ

The fifth sentence is   Ⓠ Ⓡ Ⓢ Ⓣ Ⓤ

The sixth sentence is   Ⓠ Ⓡ Ⓢ Ⓣ Ⓤ

Logical Reasoning

3. Ⓐ Ⓑ Ⓒ Ⓓ Ⓔ

4. Ⓕ Ⓖ Ⓗ Ⓙ Ⓚ

5. Ⓐ Ⓑ Ⓒ Ⓓ Ⓔ

Reading

6. Ⓕ Ⓖ Ⓗ Ⓙ Ⓚ   9. Ⓐ Ⓑ Ⓒ Ⓓ Ⓔ   12. Ⓕ Ⓖ Ⓗ Ⓙ Ⓚ

7. Ⓐ Ⓑ Ⓒ Ⓓ Ⓔ   10. Ⓕ Ⓖ Ⓗ Ⓙ Ⓚ   13. Ⓐ Ⓑ Ⓒ Ⓓ Ⓔ

8. Ⓕ Ⓖ Ⓗ Ⓙ Ⓚ   11. Ⓐ Ⓑ Ⓒ Ⓓ Ⓔ

PART II: MATHEMATICS
PROBLEM SOLVING

14. Ⓕ Ⓖ Ⓗ Ⓙ Ⓚ   19. Ⓐ Ⓑ Ⓒ Ⓓ Ⓔ   23. Ⓐ Ⓑ Ⓒ Ⓓ Ⓔ

15. Ⓐ Ⓑ Ⓒ Ⓓ Ⓔ   20. Ⓕ Ⓖ Ⓗ Ⓙ Ⓚ   24. Ⓕ Ⓖ Ⓗ Ⓙ Ⓚ

16. Ⓕ Ⓖ Ⓗ Ⓙ Ⓚ   21. Ⓐ Ⓑ Ⓒ Ⓓ Ⓔ   25. Ⓐ Ⓑ Ⓒ Ⓓ Ⓔ

17. Ⓐ Ⓑ Ⓒ Ⓓ Ⓔ   22. Ⓕ Ⓖ Ⓗ Ⓙ Ⓚ   26. Ⓕ Ⓖ Ⓗ Ⓙ Ⓚ

18. Ⓕ Ⓖ Ⓗ Ⓙ Ⓚ

answer sheet

Practice Test 3

PART 1: VERBAL

13 Questions • 20 Minutes
QUESTIONS 1–2: SCRAMBLED PARAGRAPHS

Directions: The paragraph below consists of six sentences in scrambled order. The first, or topic, sentence is given, and you are to arrange the rest in an order that makes sense, each sentence following from the one before in that it explains the earlier one or adds to it.

Write the numbers to the left of the letters (in pencil so you can change them as often as you need). When you are satisfied, mark your choices on the answer sheet.

Because you get no partial credit for having only some of the sentences in a paragraph in order and because trying different arrangements to find which reads best requires more time than other test questions, each of the scrambled paragraphs carries twice the weight of other questions on the test.

1. Humans like to categorize: to give names to things and ideas, to put like with like, and having done so, to draw conclusions.

_____**Q.** Politicians are often endomorphs; athletes and firemen, mesomorphs; while writers and computer programmers are likely ectomorphs.

_____**R.** From early times on, scientists have divided people (most often male people) into three body types and attributed behavior patterns accordingly.

_____**S.** In actuality, most of us are a combination of types, but that need not detract from the fun of fitting our acquaintances and ourselves into one or another of these categories.

_____**T.** While the names and descriptions have changed slightly over the years, what persists are the three basic descriptions.

_____**U.** Briefly, these are as follows: Endomorph—thick-bodied, food-loving, outgoing, somewhat lazy; Mesomorph—broad-shouldered, big-muscled, energetic, athletic; and Ectomorph—long, thin body, brainy, often academic (a person who prefers thought to action).

The second sentence is   Ⓠ Ⓡ Ⓢ Ⓣ Ⓤ
The third sentence is   Ⓠ Ⓡ Ⓢ Ⓣ Ⓤ
The fourth sentence is   Ⓠ Ⓡ Ⓢ Ⓣ Ⓤ
The fifth sentence is   Ⓠ Ⓡ Ⓢ Ⓣ Ⓤ
The sixth sentence is   Ⓠ Ⓡ Ⓢ Ⓣ Ⓤ

2. The First Amendment to the Constitution, which states that Congress may not make laws establishing or preventing any religion, seems clear enough, yet through the years thousands of hours of lawyers' and judges' time and millions of dollars have been spent on trying to interpret or even get around it.

_____**Q.** More recently, the problem of school prayer, even silent praying, in public schools has become a political campaign issue at least every four years.

_____**R.** Likewise, the distribution of textbooks by state boards to parochial schools—even nonreligious books—has been opposed, along with the right of parochial school students to receive state-funded remedial help.

_____**S.** The public busing of children to religious schools, which has been banned in some states but approved by the U.S. Supreme Court, has led to constant legal battles.

_____**T.** President Bush has brought a new challenge to the amendment in his effort to permit government funding to religious organizations for use in charitable work.

_____**U.** One problem arises from the fact that the amendment pertains only to the federal, not state governments.

The second sentence is   Ⓠ Ⓡ Ⓢ Ⓣ Ⓤ

The third sentence is   Ⓠ Ⓡ Ⓢ Ⓣ Ⓤ

The fourth sentence is   Ⓠ Ⓡ Ⓢ Ⓣ Ⓤ

The fifth sentence is   Ⓠ Ⓡ Ⓢ Ⓣ Ⓤ

The sixth sentence is   Ⓠ Ⓡ Ⓢ Ⓣ Ⓤ

QUESTIONS 3–5: LOGICAL REASONING

Directions: Read each question very carefully and choose the **best** answer from the five choices given. Select your answer based **only** on the information provided.

3. One day this week, Letisha went to the doctor, ate lunch at her favorite restaurant, and had her hair cut. The restaurant is open Tuesday through Saturday. The hairdresser is closed Sunday, Monday, and Tuesday. The doctor has hours on Monday, Tuesday, and Thursday. What day of the week did Letisha do all these things?

   A. Monday

   B. Tuesday

   C. Wednesday

   D. Thursday

   E. Friday

4. Cali and JoJo are not the same sex, but they have the same mother. Piper and Imu were married and later got divorced. JoJo and Piper got married, and Piper gave birth to twins. If all this is true, then it is possible that

   F. JoJo is Imu's sister.

   G. Imu is Cali's sister.

   H. JoJo is Piper's sister.

   J. Imu is JoJo's brother.

   K. Cali is Imu's brother.

The problem below uses a code where one letter stands for a word and only that word. Each line of letters represents the specific words in the line directly below. A letter may or may not appear directly above the word it codes for.

(1) F G O P R Q H K means

Bats are small and live in tall trees.

(2) S R O L P means

Trees are sturdy and hard.

(3) R U T N F M means

Short trees are free of bats.

5. Which letter could represent the word *bats*?

A. G

B. R

C. P

D. F

E. O

QUESTIONS 6–13: READING PASSAGES

Directions: Read each passage below and answer the questions that follow. Remember to **use only the information you have read in the passage** when answering the questions; you may reread the passage if necessary.

Four billion years ago, the earth's atmosphere contained no oxygen in usable form. The oxygen was combined chemically with other elements which
5 made it unavailable for breathing. It is believed that not until green plants grew on earth, providing photosynthesis, a product of which is the gas now known as oxygen, did the earth's air contain that
10 most important gas in its uncombined pure form.

We don't have concrete proof of this, because we have been unable to find prehistoric air trapped in anything. Even
15 air contained in ancient mummy tombs, assuming we could release it for study without losing it, is not really old in terms of our planet's existence.

Geologists have been learning about
20 the young earth for hundreds of years by examining its present formations, and since we have learned that chemical laws don't change with time, we can make assumptions based on those laws.
25 We therefore assume that when the earth first formed, it was formidably hot; hot enough to boil away what water existed. Consequently, we must assume that all the water on the earth today was
30 concentrated then in the atmosphere.

When the rocks covering the earth's surface finally cooled below 212 degrees Fahrenheit, the boiling point, and the air cooled along with them, all the water in
35 the air condensed into droplets, which grew in size as the molecules joined together. They got so heavy they fell, producing rain. It is believed it then rained for more than one hundred million years,
40 at the end of which we had oceans, rivers, lakes . . . fresh and clear, devoid of salt or marine animals or other forms of life.

When it finally stopped raining, the air, its oxygen bound up with other chemicals, also contained ammonia, methane, carbon dioxide, and other substances inimical to living things. In time, some of these gases dissolved in the water and brought about the first organic molecules, permitting the formation of primitive non-oxygen-breathing forms of life. The green plants that expelled oxygen came later, and when the air contained sufficient oxygen, higher forms of life made their entrance.

6. Which of the following best describes what this passage is about?

    F. How oxygen got into the earth's atmosphere

    G. How things were in ancient times

    H. What we learn about air from chemistry

    J. Where our oceans come from

    K. How photosynthesis uses chemicals

7. According to the passage, we can assume that

    A. photosynthesis is carried out by all living things.

    B. the boiling temperature of water has changed over billions of years.

    C. water became salty because of the constant rain.

    D. the earth's surface was much hotter billions of years ago.

    E. chemical laws will change over time.

8. The process of photosynthesis

    F. permitted the formation of primitive life forms.

    G. produced an assortment of gases.

    H. uses methane to produce oxides.

    J. was a product of early oxygen consumption.

    K. releases oxygen into the air.

9. Which of the following can be inferred about the primitive atmosphere?

    A. It was unfit for breathing.

    B. It is hidden in undiscovered places, such as glaciers.

    C. It will someday be found to be poisonous to primitive life.

    D. It contains pure oxygen.

    E. It was devoid of water vapor.

During the years of Communist rule in the Soviet Union, 12-year-old Walter Polovchak and his parents, all Russian-born, escaped to America and were granted irrevocable asylum in this country. Shortly after their escape, Walter's parents became homesick and decided to return to Russia.

But Walter, who had become like an American, valued the freedom of life in America. Rather than return with his parents, he ran secretly to the home of some distant American relatives and, with their help, managed to retain the services of a Ukrainian-born lawyer. An East Coast lawyer and her husband, a professor of constitutional law, also became involved, and all of them working "pro bono" (for nothing) fought for Walter's right to stay in America.

Surprisingly, the American Civil Liberties Union (ACLU) fought on the parents' side to revoke Walter's asylum and deport him in the name of "integrity of the family," which is how the Soviets saw it.

Walter knew that if he was forced to return, "they put me in jail or to a mental house." His lawyers said that at the least he would have been drugged or bullied until he was purged of his ideas.

The story ended happily for Walter after years of legal battle, when he was eighteen, and graduated from high school here. By now a popular, happy American boy, he took the oath of citizenship in Washington, while his lawyers, loving relatives, and school friends cheered for him.

10. Which of the following is the best headline for this passage?

   F. Russian Boy Defies Parents to Become American

   G. ACLU Helps Boy Stay Home

   H. Family Values Triumph

   J. Getting Free Lawyers Is Easy

   K. American Runaway

11. If Walter had been sent back to Russia,

   A. he would have been shot.

   B. he would have been a hero.

   C. he would have been treated as if he were insane.

   D. he would have gone to school.

   E. his parents would have been angry.

12. How many lawyers helped Walter?

   F. None

   G. Three

   H. An entire law firm

   J. Several ACLU lawyers

   K. Five

13. From the Soviet point of view, what had Walter done wrong?

   A. He ran away.

   B. He used a Ukrainian lawyer.

   C. He defied his parents.

   D. He liked school here.

   E. He had come to America.

PART II: MATHEMATICS

13 Questions • 20 Minutes

The following information is provided for your reference. It will likely not appear in the actual test booklet. You should memorize these formulas and symbols.

FORMULAS

- Area of a circle (with radius r) $= \pi r^2$

- Circumference of a circle $= 2\pi r$

- Area of a parallelogram (with base b and height h) $= bh$

- Area of a trapezoid (with parallel sides a and b and height h) $= \frac{1}{2}(a+b)h$

- Volume of a cone or pyramid (with base area b and height h) $= \frac{1}{3}bh$

- Volume of a cylinder (with base area b and height h) $= bh$

- Volume of a sphere $\left(\text{with radius } r\right) = \frac{4}{3}\pi r^3$

- Sum of the measures of the angles of a triangle $= 180°$

- Area of a triangle:

$$\text{Area} = \frac{bh}{2}$$

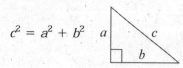

- For a right triangle:

$$c^2 = a^2 + b^2$$

DEFINITIONS OF SYMBOLS

$=$ is equal to

$\neq$ is unequal to

$<$ is less than

$>$ is greater than

$\leq$ is less than or equal to

$\geq$ is greater than or equal to

$\perp$ is perpendicular to

$\parallel$ is parallel to

$\angle$ angle

$\llcorner$ right angle

$\rightrightarrows$ parallel lines

NOTES

- Figures may not be drawn to scale. Do not assume any relationship in a diagram unless it is specifically stated or can be figured out from given information.

- Assume that a diagram is in one plane unless the problem specifically states that it is not.

- Reduce all fractions to lowest terms.

QUESTIONS 14–26: PROBLEM SOLVING

Directions: For each question, solve the problem and select the best answer from the choices given.

14. If $\boxed{x} = \dfrac{1}{x^2}$, then $\boxed{2} + \boxed{3} =$

    F. $\dfrac{13}{36}$

    G. $\dfrac{1}{5}$

    H. $\dfrac{5}{6}$

    J. $\dfrac{1}{8}$

    K. $\dfrac{5}{13}$

15. There are 30 students in a class, and 18 of them are boys. What percent of the class is girls?

    A. 60%

    B. 0.60

    C. 40%

    D. 0.45

    E. 12

16. The area of a square rug with sides that are 3 feet long each is

    F. 81 in.²

    G. 108 in.²

    H. 243 in.²

    J. 708 in.²

    K. 1296 in.²

17. $19\dfrac{1}{4} - 7\dfrac{1}{3} =$

    A. $10\dfrac{1}{4}$

    B. $11\dfrac{11}{12}$

    C. 0.0025

    D. 2.5

    E. 25

18. $\dfrac{\sqrt{80}}{8}$ is between

    F. 0 and 1

    G. 1 and 2

    H. 2 and 3

    J. 3 and 4

    K. 4 and 5

19. Two numbers are in the ratio of 2:3. If the larger number is 45, the smaller number is

    A. 30

    B. $67\dfrac{1}{2}$

    C. 15

    D. $22\dfrac{1}{2}$

    E. 12

20. If the area of a circle is 314 square inches, then its circumference is closest to: (use $\pi = 3.14$)

    F. 58 cm

    G. 60 cm

    H. 63 cm

    J. 65 cm

    K. 68 cm

21.

A ———————— B ———————————— C
    2x   3x

If the ratio of AB to BC is 2:3, then what percent is BC of AC?

A. 55%

B. 67%

C. 65%

D. 60%

E. 40%

22. If 2% of a number is 10, then 50% of that same number is

F. 500

G. 250

H. 100

J. 50

K. 0.1

23. The following triangles are similar. Find the missing side that is labeled x.

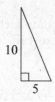 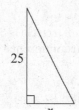

A. 2.5

B. 7.5

C. 15

D. 22.5

E. 12.5

24. 140% of 70 is

F. 0.98

G. 9.8

H. 98

J. 150

K. 9800

25.

	5 gallons	2 quarts	1 pint
−	1 gallon	3 quarts	

A. 2 gal. 2 qt. 1 pt.

B. 2 gal. 6 qt. 2 pt.

C. 3 gal. 3 qt. 1 pt.

D. 4 gal. 3 qt. 1 pt.

E. 4 gal. 9 qt. 1 pt.

26. In the fraction $\dfrac{xy}{z}$, if the value of z is doubled and the value of x is halved, the value of the fraction is

F. multiplied by four.

G. decreased by $\dfrac{1}{2}$

H. increased by $\dfrac{1}{2}$

J. doubled.

K. divided by four.

ANSWER KEY AND EXPLANATIONS

1. RTUQS	7. D	12. G	17. B	22. G
2. USRQT	8. K	13. C	18. G	23. E
3. D	9. A	14. F	19. A	24. H
4. J	10. F	15. C	20. H	25. C
5. D	11. C	16. K	21. D	26. K
6. F				

PART I: VERBAL
SCRAMBLED PARAGRAPHS

1. **The correct order is RTUQS.** R is the second sentence because it takes the lead sentence further, mentioning one area of categorization. T is third because it carries on generally about the area of categorization mentioned in the second sentence. U is fourth because it continues to expand more from the first two sentences, naming and describing the three types. Q is fifth because it gives examples of the types in the sentence before. S is sixth because it refers back to the topic sentence.

2. **The correct order is USRQT.** U is the second sentence because it gives an example of the problems that have come from the amendment. S is third because a problem with application of the amendment by states follows the first reference to state. R is fourth because, starting with "likewise," it must connect in some way to the third sentence. Q is fifth because it begins with "more recently" and continues by listing another problem for state governments. T is sixth because it brings the problem up to date.

LOGICAL REASONING

3. **The correct answer is D.** You needn't worry about Saturday and Sunday because they are not choices. Set up a table of days *open* for each activity (see below). Thursday is the only day all three are open.

Doctor	Hairdresser	Restaurant
Mon.		
Tues.		Tues.
	Wed.	Wed.
Thurs.	Thurs.	Thurs.
	Fri.	Fri.

4. **The correct answer is J.** Write down the names of the people. First you are told that Cali and JoJo are brother and sister—write it down. Since Piper and Imu were married, one is male and the other is female—write it down. The next sentence tells you that Piper is a female and that she married JoJo, who therefore is a male—write it down. Now you know that Cali is a female, and Imu is a male. Choice J is the only correct answer.

Sentence 1		Sentence 2		Sentence 3
Cali	JoJo	Piper	Imu	. . . makes it evident that Piper
Sister ↔ Brother		Husband ↔ Wife		is the female, so JoJo is the
Brother ↔ Sister		Husband ↔ Husband		male. Therefore, Cali is female
Female ↔ Male		Female ↔ Male		and Imu is male. Put it down
				on the diagram

5. **The correct answer is D.** *Bats* appears in sentence 1 and sentence 3. If you check all the answer choices G, R, P, F, and O you will see that only F appears in sentence 1 and sentence 3. The only choice is F which is answer D.

READING PASSAGES

6. **The correct answer is F.** The passage starts with the question of where oxygen in the air came from and ends with the answer. All of the other answers have a place in the passage, yet each is only contributory to the main question.

7. **The correct answer is D.** Paragraph four states that the earth's surface was a lot hotter in the past. Regarding choices A, B, C, and E, photosynthesis is restricted to green plants. Chemical laws do not change, so water will boil at the same temperature. Nothing is mentioned about the present salt content of the oceans.

8. **The correct answer is K.** Photosynthesis releases oxygen into the air as stated in the first paragraph. Choice F is wrong; it was higher life forms that depended on oxygen. Choices G, H, and J are nowhere corroborated in the passage.

9. **The correct answer is A.** The last paragraph states that oxygen came with the green plants, and then came higher forms of life, which can be assumed to breathe oxygen. Choice B may give you a moment's thought, yet glaciers are frozen water and came much later—after the earth cooled. Choice C doesn't hold up because primitive life developed in the primitive atmosphere. Choices D and E are wrong because the passage states the opposite.

10. **The correct answer is F.** If this were a newspaper headline, the first option describes the story. Choices G, H, and J are untrue to the story, and choice K is wrong because Walter was not an American when he ran away from his parents.

11. **The correct answer is C.** Choice A is wrong because it is not in the story. Choice D. is probably true but never mentioned. Choices B and E are the exact opposite of the truth. That leaves choice C, which is what Walter feared.

12. **The correct answer is G.** Choice G is correct: the Ukrainian lawyer, the East Coast woman, and her lawyer husband. Choice J is wrong because the ACLU lawyers were on the side of Walter's parents.

13. **The correct answer is C.** While they probably did not like any of the possibilities, the only one stated in the passage is choice C.

Part II: Mathematics

PROBLEM SOLVING

14. The correct answer is F. $\boxed{2} + \boxed{3} = \dfrac{1}{2^2} + \dfrac{1}{3^2} = \dfrac{1}{4} + \dfrac{1}{9} = \dfrac{9}{36} + \dfrac{4}{36} = \dfrac{13}{36}$

15. The correct answer is C. $30 - 18 = 12$ girls

$$\dfrac{12}{30} = 30\overline{)12.00}^{\,.40}$$

$.40 = 40\%$

16. The correct answer is K.

$A = l \times w$

$A = 36 \times 36 = 1\ 296$ in.^{2}

17. The correct answer is B.

$$
\begin{array}{llll}
19\dfrac{1}{4} = & 19\dfrac{3}{12} = & 18\dfrac{3}{12} + \dfrac{12}{12} = & 18\dfrac{15}{12} \\[3mm]
-\ 7\dfrac{1}{3} = & -\ 7\dfrac{4}{12} = & -\ 7\dfrac{4}{12} \quad = & -\ 7\dfrac{4}{12} \\[2mm]
\hline
& & & 11\dfrac{11}{12}
\end{array}
$$

18. The correct answer is G.

$\dfrac{\sqrt{80}}{8}$ lies between $\dfrac{\sqrt{64}}{8}$ and $\dfrac{\sqrt{81}}{8}$

$\dfrac{\sqrt{80}}{8}$ lies between $\dfrac{8}{8}$ and $\dfrac{9}{8}$

$\dfrac{\sqrt{80}}{8}$ lies between 1 and $1\dfrac{1}{8}$

19. The correct answer is A. $\dfrac{2}{3} = \dfrac{x}{45}$ since two equal ratios form a proportion.

$2 \times 45 = 3 \times x.$ (Cross products of a proportion are equal.)

$\quad 90 = 3x$

$\quad 90 = x$

20. The correct answer is H. The area of a circle is $A = \pi r^2$. Thus,

$$\pi r^2 = 314$$
$$3.14\,r^2 = 314$$
$$r^2 = 100$$
$$r = 10$$

The circumference of a circle is $C = 2\pi r$. So, $C = 2\pi(10) = (2)(3.14)(10) = 62.8$ in.

21. The correct answer is D.

The ratio of BC:AC is $\dfrac{3x}{5x} = \dfrac{3}{5}$

Thus, BC is 60% of AC

22. The correct answer is G.

$$2\% \text{ of } x = 10$$
$$.02\,x = 10 \qquad 50\% \text{ of } 500 = 500$$
$$2x = 1000 \qquad\qquad \times\ .50$$
$$x = 500 \qquad\qquad 250.00$$

23. The correct answer is E. If two triangles are similar, then their sides are in proportion. Thus,

$$\frac{10}{25} = \frac{5}{x}$$
$$10x = 125$$
$$x = 12.5$$

24. The correct answer is H. This is a good problem to do in your head. Note that 10% of 70 is 7. 140%, then, is 14×7, or 98.

25. The correct answer is C. Borrow a gallon and add it to 2 quarts. Rewrite the problem. Remember that you borrowed.

	4 gallons	6 quarts	1 pint
−	1 gallon	3 quarts	0 pints
	3 gallons	3 quarts	1 pint

26. The correct answer is K. By doubling the denominator of a fraction, we actually divide it by two. By halving one of the factors in the numerator, we also halve the value of the fraction. By doing both, we have actually divided the original value by four. Plug in some values for x, y, and z, and try this yourself.

ANSWER SHEET PRACTICE TEST 4
Part I: Verbal

Scrambled Paragraphs

Paragraph 1

The second sentence is Ⓠ Ⓡ Ⓢ Ⓣ Ⓤ

The third sentence is Ⓠ Ⓡ Ⓢ Ⓣ Ⓤ

The fourth sentence is Ⓠ Ⓡ Ⓢ Ⓣ Ⓤ

The fifth sentence is Ⓠ Ⓡ Ⓢ Ⓣ Ⓤ

The sixth sentence is Ⓠ Ⓡ Ⓢ Ⓣ Ⓤ

Paragraph 2

The second sentence is Ⓠ Ⓡ Ⓢ Ⓣ Ⓤ

The third sentence is Ⓠ Ⓡ Ⓢ Ⓣ Ⓤ

The fourth sentence is Ⓠ Ⓡ Ⓢ Ⓣ Ⓤ

The fifth sentence is Ⓠ Ⓡ Ⓢ Ⓣ Ⓤ

The sixth sentence is Ⓠ Ⓡ Ⓢ Ⓣ Ⓤ

Logical Reasoning

3. Ⓐ Ⓑ Ⓒ Ⓓ Ⓔ

4. Ⓕ Ⓖ Ⓗ Ⓙ Ⓚ

5. Ⓐ Ⓑ Ⓒ Ⓓ Ⓔ

Reading

6. Ⓕ Ⓖ Ⓗ Ⓙ Ⓚ

7. Ⓐ Ⓑ Ⓒ Ⓓ Ⓔ

8. Ⓕ Ⓖ Ⓗ Ⓙ Ⓚ

9. Ⓐ Ⓑ Ⓒ Ⓓ Ⓔ

10. Ⓕ Ⓖ Ⓗ Ⓙ Ⓚ

11. Ⓐ Ⓑ Ⓒ Ⓓ Ⓔ

12. Ⓕ Ⓖ Ⓗ Ⓙ Ⓚ

13. Ⓐ Ⓑ Ⓒ Ⓓ Ⓔ

PART II: MATHEMATICS
PROBLEM SOLVING

14. Ⓕ Ⓖ Ⓗ Ⓙ Ⓚ

15. Ⓐ Ⓑ Ⓒ Ⓓ Ⓔ

16. Ⓕ Ⓖ Ⓗ Ⓙ Ⓚ

17. Ⓐ Ⓑ Ⓒ Ⓓ Ⓔ

18. Ⓕ Ⓖ Ⓗ Ⓙ Ⓚ

19. Ⓐ Ⓑ Ⓒ Ⓓ Ⓔ

20. Ⓕ Ⓖ Ⓗ Ⓙ Ⓚ

21. Ⓐ Ⓑ Ⓒ Ⓓ Ⓔ

22. Ⓕ Ⓖ Ⓗ Ⓙ Ⓚ

23. Ⓐ Ⓑ Ⓒ Ⓓ Ⓔ

24. Ⓕ Ⓖ Ⓗ Ⓙ Ⓚ

25. Ⓐ Ⓑ Ⓒ Ⓓ Ⓔ

26. Ⓕ Ⓖ Ⓗ Ⓙ Ⓚ

answer sheet

Practice Test 4

PART 1: VERBAL

13 Questions • 20 Minutes

QUESTIONS 1–2: SCRAMBLED PARAGRAPHS

Directions: The paragraph below consists of six sentences in scrambled order. The first, or topic, sentence is given, and you are to arrange the rest in an order that makes sense, each sentence following from the one before in that it explains the earlier one or adds to it.

Write the numbers to the left of the letters (in pencil so you can change them as often as you need). When you are satisfied, mark your choices on the answer sheet.

Because you get no partial credit for having only some of the sentences in a paragraph in order and because trying different arrangements to find which reads best requires more time than other test questions, each of the scrambled paragraphs carries twice the weight of other questions on the test.

1. We think of skiing and skating as sports, but they did not start out that way.

_____**Q.** As long ago as two or three thousand B.C.E., skis were used to get around in snowy Scandinavian countries, and skates provided for quick, easy transportation on frozen rivers and lakes.

_____**R.** The earliest skis were made of large animal bones strapped to the feet, as we know from a five thousand-year-old pair in a Swedish museum.

_____**S.** Skis were used by the Scandinavian soldiers as long ago as 1200 C.E., both for spying and transporting troops across the snow-covered mountains.

_____**T.** During World War II, long, wooden skis, painted as camouflage, were used by our Tenth Mountain Division soldiers who trained to fight in snowy mountains—something most never got to do.

_____**U.** By the eighteenth century, on much-improved equipment, skating was taken up for sport, followed by skiing on wood skis in the 19th century.

The second sentence is   Ⓠ Ⓡ Ⓢ Ⓣ Ⓤ
The third sentence is   Ⓠ Ⓡ Ⓢ Ⓣ Ⓤ
The fourth sentence is   Ⓠ Ⓡ Ⓢ Ⓣ Ⓤ
The fifth sentence is   Ⓠ Ⓡ Ⓢ Ⓣ Ⓤ
The sixth sentence is   Ⓠ Ⓡ Ⓢ Ⓣ Ⓤ

2. A serious flaw in our supposedly democratic electoral system is the cost of winning a campaign.

_____**Q.** Historically, legislation designed to correct this abuse has been turned down by the very politicians whose greed is the target.

_____**R.** Unfortunately, the bulk of this money comes from special-interest groups and corporations seeking future favors.

_____**S.** The current campaign finance reform bill is by no means assured of passage—or even to be politician-proof if it does manage to squeak through.

_____**T.** By 1994, the average winning Senator spent $4.6 million, and the average winning congressman, of whom there are so many more, spent about half a million campaigning.

_____**U.** Each candidate running for election or reelection to either house must solicit advertising money in ever-increasing amounts as costs go up.

The second sentence is Ⓠ Ⓡ Ⓢ Ⓣ Ⓤ
The third sentence is Ⓠ Ⓡ Ⓢ Ⓣ Ⓤ
The fourth sentence is Ⓠ Ⓡ Ⓢ Ⓣ Ⓤ
The fifth sentence is Ⓠ Ⓡ Ⓢ Ⓣ Ⓤ
The sixth sentence is Ⓠ Ⓡ Ⓢ Ⓣ Ⓤ

QUESTIONS 3–5: LOGICAL REASONING

Directions: Read each question very carefully and choose the **best** answer from the five choices given. Select your answer based **only** on the information provided.

3.

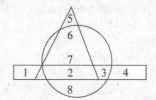

How many numbers are in the circle and also in either the triangle or the rectangle but not both?

A. 1

B. 2

C. 3

D. 4

E. 5

4. Bill and Fernando are taller than Tomas. Hernando is shorter than Bill but taller than Fernando. Going from tallest to shortest, which of the following is the correct order?

F. Bill, Fernando, Hernando, Tomas

G. Fernando, Bill, Hernando, Tomas

J. Fernando, Bill, Tomas, Hernando

J. Bill, Hernando, Fernando, Tomas

K. Hernando, Fernando, Bill, Tomas

The problem below uses a code where one specific letter stands for a word and only that word. The letter representing a word usually is *not* located directly above the word it represents. Each line of letters stands for the words in the line below.

(1) V   R   W   P   L   means
   At   seven   Kim   eats   dinner.

(2) T   V   R   U   Z   means
   Ralph   dines   Fridays   at   seven.

(3) M   Q   T   S   P   means
   Mondays   Ralph   enjoys   dinner   alone.

(4) L   W   X   V   P   means
   Kim   eats   dinner   at   home.

5. What three letters set in the proper order would mean *dinner at seven*?

A. WVR

B. VPR

C. PRV

D. PVR

E. PVW

QUESTIONS 6–13: READING PASSAGES

Directions: Read each passage below and answer the questions that follow. Remember to **use only the information you have read in the passage** when answering the questions; you may reread the passage if necessary.

Even young people have heard of osteoporosis, a fancy name for brittle bones, which affects mostly the quite elderly. When it is severe, a bone breaks,
5 causing a fall, instead of vice versa as for the rest of us.

Is there any reason for you to be interested in this condition, unless you have a brittle-boned grandparent?
10 Actually, yes. Because, believe it or not, you are going to get old, too, and if you want your bones to hold you up, you have to start living right—now.

Because women, whose bones are
15 customarily lighter than men's, are more prone to osteoporosis, teenage girls should pay extra attention to developing a healthy lifestyle.

Your bones, hard on the surface, are
20 spongy and pliable inside. In fact, they consist of 50 percent water. They must be rigid enough to bear your weight throughout life and to withstand strong forces, and yet flexible enough to permit
25 movement. Your bones take in calcium, store it, and release it when you need it.

If osteoporosis runs in your family, or your frame is smaller than average, or you are very thin, you are considered
30 at risk. But the more bone density you build in your youth, the better you will withstand bone loss later on.

So start now, if you have not already, to make weight-bearing exercise a daily
35 activity (walking, running, cycling, dancing, gardening, team sports, etc.). And keep up your calcium intake by eating lots of green leafy vegetables, bony little fish, and dairy products. Aim
40 to be the last one on your block to stand tall at eighty.

6. Which of the following best tells what this passage is about?

   F. Preventing bone loss in old age by living right while young

   G. Curing osteoporosis

   H. The difficulties of old age

   J. Why your lifestyle has nothing to do with breaking bones in old age

   K. How to live with bone disease

7. The passage claims that

   A. osteoporosis is of no concern to men.

   B. bone density is affected by climate.

   C. osteoporosis is to a degree hereditary.

   D. the more water your bones contain, the weaker the bones are.

   E. aging is preventable.

8. The passage suggests that certain foods prevent

   F. aging.

   G. the need to exercise.

   H. calcium loss.

   J. dense porosity.

   K. fat buildup.

9. According to the passage, bone breakage in the old differs from bone breakage in the young in that in the old,

   A. obesity often causes the bone to break.

   B. accidents are usually responsible for the bone break.

   C. the breaking bone causes the fall.

   D. carelessness causes most bone breaks.

   E. most bone breaks are sports related.

One night as Wahb, the young grizzly bear, wandered by the deep water, a peculiar smell reached his nose. It was quite pleasant, so he followed it up to the

5 water's edge. It seemed to come from a sunken log. As he reached over toward this, there was a sudden clank, and one of his paws was caught in a strong, steel beaver trap.

10 Wahb yelled and jerked back with all his strength, and tore up the stake that held the trap. He tried to shake it off, then ran away through the bushes trailing it. He tore at it with his teeth,

15 but there it hung, quiet, cold, strong, and immovable. Time and again he tore at it with his teeth and claws or beat it against the ground. . . . He did not know what it was, but his little greenbrown

20 eyes glazed with a mixture of pain, fright, and fury as he tried to understand his new enemy.

. . . He held it down with one paw while he tightened his teeth on the other

25 end, and bearing down as it slid away, the trap jaws opened and the foot was free. It was mere chance, of course, that led him to squeeze both springs at once. He did not understand it, but he did

30 not forget it, and he got these not very clear ideas:

"There is a dreadful little enemy that hides by the water and waits for one. It has an odd smell. It bites one's paws and

35 it is too hard for one to bite. But it can be gotten off by hard squeezing."

10. Which of the following is the best title for this passage?

   F. How to Escape a Trap

   G. The Bear Cub

   H. Wahb Encounters a New Enemy

   J. Wahb Gets Angry

   K. How to Make a Trap

11. Wahb was attracted to the trap by

    A. its bright color.

    B. the sudden clank.

    C. its strangeness.

    D. the pleasant smell.

    E. the water.

12. In reading this passage, you "suspend your disbelief" in order to accept that

    F. a bear cub could accidentally get out of a trap.

    G. a bear cub could wander alone near the water.

    H. the bear did not recognize an animal trap.

    J. the author could know what the little bear was thinking.

    K. a bear could be named Wahb.

13. Which of the following best tells what Wahb learned from the experience?

    A. Don't go out alone.

    B. A trap can be removed by hard squeezing.

    C. It is useful to have strong teeth.

    D. Don't trust things that smell good.

    E. Stay away from water.

PART II: MATHEMATICS

13 Questions • 20 Minutes

The following information is provided for your reference. It will likely not appear in the actual test booklet. You should memorize these formulas and symbols.

FORMULAS

- Area of a circle (with radius r) = πr^2

- Circumference of a circle = $2\pi r$

- Area of a parallelogram (with base b and height h) = bh

- Area of a trapezoid (with parallel sides a and b and height h) = $\frac{1}{2}(a+b)h$

- Volume of a cone or pyramid (with base area b and height h) = $\frac{1}{3}bh$

- Volume of a cylinder (with base area b and height h) = bh

- Volume of a sphere (with radius r) = $\frac{4}{3}\pi r^3$

- Sum of the measures of the angles of a triangle = 180°

- Area of a triangle:

  Area = $\frac{bh}{2}$

  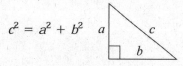

- For a right triangle:

  $c^2 = a^2 + b^2$

DEFINITIONS OF SYMBOLS

= is equal to

≠ is unequal to

< is less than

> is greater than

≤ is less than or equal to

≥ is greater than or equal to

⊥ is perpendicular to

|| is parallel to

∠ angle

∟ right angle

⇉ parallel lines

NOTES

- Figures may not be drawn to scale. Do not assume any relationship in a diagram unless it is specifically stated or can be figured out from given information.

- Assume that a diagram is in one plane unless the problem specifically states that it is not.

- Reduce all fractions to lowest terms.

QUESTIONS 14–26: PROBLEM SOLVING

Directions: For each question, solve the problem and select the best answer from the choices given.

14. $|4 - 7| - |3 - 8| =$

   F. 0

   G. 8

   H. 2

   J. –2

   K. –4

15. If $\frac{1}{3}$ of a number is 12, $\frac{1}{2}$ of the same number is

   A. 36

   B. 72

   C. 18

   D. 6

   E. 2

16. The number whose value is closest to 1 is

   F. $\frac{7}{8}$

   G. $1\frac{1}{8}$

   H. 1.09

   J. 0.89

   K. $\frac{9}{10}$

17.

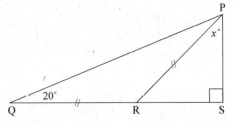

In the figure above, PR = QR. What is the measure of angle x?

   A. 50

   B. 40

   C. 60

   D. 20

   E. Cannot be determined

18. $66\frac{2}{3}\%$ of $\frac{2}{3}$ is

   F. $\frac{1}{3}$

   G. $\frac{4}{9}$

   H. $\frac{2}{3}$

   J. $1\frac{1}{3}$

   K. 1

19. $\dfrac{7 \times 6 \times 5 \times 4 \times 3}{21 \times 10} =$

   A. $\frac{35}{2}$

   B. 12

   C. 30

   D. $\frac{5}{3}$

   E. 42

20. What is the sum of the odd factors of 30?

   F. 9

   G. 11

   H. 12

   J. 23

   K. 24

21. What is the value of $\dfrac{a^3}{b^2}$ if $a = -2$ and $b = -4$?

    A. -2

    B. $-\dfrac{1}{4}$

    C. $-\dfrac{1}{2}$

    D. 2

    E. 4

22. Solve for x: $9 - \dfrac{3}{x} = 4$

    F. $\dfrac{3}{5}$

    G. $\dfrac{1}{3}$

    H. 1

    J. $\dfrac{4}{9}$

    K. 3

23.

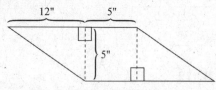

What is the perimeter of the parallelogram shown above?

    A. 20"

    B. 35"

    C. 60"

    D. 30"

    E. None of these

24. To find the radius of a circle whose circumference is 60 inches,

    F. multiply 60 by π.

    G. divide 60 by 2π.

    H. divide 30 by 2π

    J. divide 60 by π and extract the square root of the result.

    K. multiply 60 by $\dfrac{\pi}{2}$.

25. A carpenter needs four boards, each 2 feet 9 inches long. If wood is sold only by the foot, how many feet must he buy?

    A. 9

    B. 10

    C. 11

    D. 12

    E. 13

26. The approximate distance, S, in feet that an object falls in t seconds when dropped from a height can be found by using the formula $S = 16t^2$. In 8 seconds, the object will fall

    F. 256 feet.

    G. 1024 feet.

    H. 1084 feet.

    J. 2048 feet.

    K. 15,384 feet.

ANSWER KEY AND EXPLANATIONS

1. QRSUT	7. C	12. J	17. A	22. F
2. UTRQS	8. D	13. B	18. G	23. C
3. C	9. C	14. J	19. B	24. G
4. J	10. H	15. C	20. K	25. C
5. D	11. D	16. H	21. C	26. G
6. F				

PART I: VERBAL
SCRAMBLED PARAGRAPHS

1. **The correct order is QRSUT.** Q is the second sentence because it continues the thought "they did not start out" from the topic sentence. R is third because it goes on about skis from several thousand years ago. S is fourth because the time is brought forward by not as far in the remaining two sentences. U is fifth because it continues to move ahead in time. T is sixth because as the most recent use described in the paragraph, it concludes it.

2. **The correct order is UTRQS.** U is the second sentence because it describes the flaw mentioned in the topic sentence. T is third because it details the cost mentioned in the second sentence. R is fourth because "this money" has to refer back to the third sentence. Q is fifth because it mentions why the condition continues. S is sixth because it refers to the present attempt to cure the condition in the fifth sentence.

LOGICAL REASONING

3. **The correct answer is C.** Find the numbers in the circle: 6, 7, 2, 3, and 8. Eliminate 2 because it is in both the triangle and the rectangle. Eliminate 8 because it is not in either the triangle or the rectangle. That leaves three numbers: 6, 7, and 3.

4. **The correct answer is J.** Put down the names of the four boys in any order along a vertical line: Bill, Fernando, Hernando, Tomas. Now take the information in the first sentence and adjust the four names going from tallest to shortest. Since Bill and Fernando are taller than Tomas, no change has yet to be made in your list. Next, look at sentence two and adjust your list. This puts Hernando between Bill and Fernando: Bill, Hernando, Fernando, Tomas. Now check the choices and find the one that fits your diagram: choice J is correct.

5. **The correct answer is D.** One method for attacking this problem is to find the letter standing for *dinner*. The word *dinner* appears in the first, third, and fourth sentence. By eliminating all those letters above sentence 1 that do not appear in sentences 1, 3, and 4, you are left with the letter P, this eliminates choices A and B. Now, you are left with choices C, D, and E, the only choices that begin with the word *dinner*. Focus on the second word *at*, it is found in sentences 1, 2, and 4. Also notice that sentence 1 contains all the words for which you are being asked to determine the letters. The only letter appearing in sentences 1, 2, and 4 is V so it must stand out for *at*. Now you have PV; you need to find the code for the last word *seven*, it appears in sentences 1 and 2, the only letter appearing in sentences 1 and 2 is the letter R, therefore, it must code for the word *seven*.

READING PASSAGES

6. **The correct answer is F.** The entire passage concerns osteoporosis and how developing a healthy lifestyle when you're young can help to prevent osteoporosis when you're old. Choice G is wrong because you can't cure osteoporosis. Choice J is wrong because it is the opposite of what the passage says, and choices J and K are not discussed.

7. **The correct answer is C.** The next-to-last paragraph states that osteoporosis in the family puts you at risk, and this suggests a hereditary connection. Choice A is not true. Choices B, D, and E are not mentioned in the passage.

8. **The correct answer is H.** The last paragraph mentions keeping up your calcium intake as a preventative measure. This suggests fairly directly that calcium loss is related to osteoporosis. Calcium is also mentioned as a bone substance in paragraph five.

9. **The correct answer is C.** Bone breakage causing a fall is described in paragraph one as a consequence of osteoporosis. All other causes are true of young people as well as old people.

10. **The correct answer is H.** Although choices F and J are discussed in the passage, they are not the main idea. Choice J encompasses the whole topic, and so is the best title. Choice G is not specific enough, and choice K is not discussed.

11. **The correct answer is D.** The only choice mentioned is D, the smell.

12. **The correct answer is J.** To "suspend disbelief" is a literary term referring, as it sounds, to going along with a story or fantasy. You can easily accept that a bear could F escape a trap, G wander alone near the water, or J not recognize a trap. Choice K is a little trickier—who names a bear, but if someone does, any name is possible. That leaves the correct choice, J, which is of course impossible, but believing this is important to the passage.

13. **The correct answer is B.** We can't figure out for ourselves what the bear learned, so the only correct choice is B, which is what the passage says he learned.

Part II: Mathematics

PROBLEM SOLVING

14. The correct answer is J. $|4 - 7| - |3 - 8| = |-3| - |-5| = 3 - 5 = -2$

15. The correct answer is C. Let x = the number. Therefore, $\frac{1}{3}x = 12$

Multiply by 3: $3\left(\frac{1}{3}x\right) = (12)3$

$$x = 36$$

$$\frac{1}{2} \text{ of } 36 = 18$$

16. The correct answer is H.

$$\frac{7}{8} = 0.875 = 0.125 \text{ less than } 1$$

$$1\frac{1}{8} = 1.125 = 0.125 \text{ more than } 1$$

$$\frac{9}{10} = 0.900 = 0.100 \text{ less than } 1$$

$$0.89 = 0.890 = 0.110 \text{ less than } 1$$

$$1.09 = 1.090 = 0.090 \text{ more than } 1 \text{ (closest to 1)}$$

17. The correct answer is A. In a triangle, if two sides are equal, then the angles opposite these sides have the same measure.

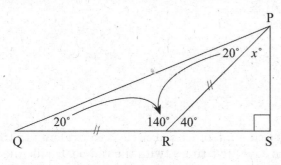

$$40 + 90 + x = 180$$

$$130 + x = 180$$

$$x = 50$$

18. The correct answer is G. $66\frac{2}{3}\% = \frac{2}{3}$ as a fraction. Therefore, $\frac{2}{3} \times \frac{2}{3} = \frac{4}{9}$.

19. The correct answer is B. There is no need to multiply out the numerator and denominator; just reduce the fraction the way it's given:

$$\frac{\cancel{7} \times 6 \times 5 \times 4 \times \cancel{3}}{\cancel{21} \times 10} = \frac{6 \times 5 \times 4^2}{{}_5\cancel{10}} = \frac{6 \times \cancel{5} \times 2}{\cancel{5}} = 12$$

20. **The correct answer is K.** The factors of 30 are 1, 2, 3, 5, 6, 10, 15, 30.

    The sum of the odd factors is $1 + 3 + 5 + 15 = 24$.

21. **The correct answer is C.** If $a = -2$, $b = -4$, then

    $$\frac{a^3}{b^2} = \frac{(-2)^3}{(-4)^2} = \frac{-8}{16} = -\frac{1}{2}$$

22. **The correct answer is F.**

    $$9 - \frac{3}{x} = 4 \qquad \frac{3}{x} = \frac{5}{1}$$

    $$5 - \frac{3}{x} = 0 \qquad 5x = 3$$

    $$x = \frac{3}{5}$$

23. **The correct answer is C.**

    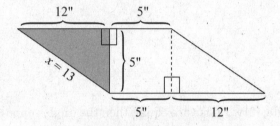

    Use the Pythagorean theorem to find x:

    $x^2 = 5^2 + 12^2$

    $x^2 = 25 + 144$

    $x^2 = 169$

    $x = 13$

    Perimeter = $17 + 13 + 17 + 13 = 60$

24. **The correct answer is G.** Because the circumference of a circle is equivalent to π times the diameter, the circumference is also equal to π times twice the radius. Divide the circumference by 2π.

25. **The correct answer is C.** Four boards, each 2'9" long, total 11 feet. The carpenter must buy 11 feet of wood.

26. **The correct answer is G.** Find the answer to this problem by substituting the values given into the formula.

    $S = 16t^2$

    $S = 16(8)2 = 16(64) = 1024$ feet

ANSWER SHEET PRACTICE TEST 5
Part I: Verbal

Scrambled Paragraphs

Paragraph 1

The second sentence is Ⓠ Ⓡ Ⓢ Ⓣ Ⓤ

The third sentence is Ⓠ Ⓡ Ⓢ Ⓣ Ⓤ

The fourth sentence is Ⓠ Ⓡ Ⓢ Ⓣ Ⓤ

The fifth sentence is Ⓠ Ⓡ Ⓢ Ⓣ Ⓤ

The sixth sentence is Ⓠ Ⓡ Ⓢ Ⓣ Ⓤ

Paragraph 2

The second sentence is Ⓠ Ⓡ Ⓢ Ⓣ Ⓤ

The third sentence is Ⓠ Ⓡ Ⓢ Ⓣ Ⓤ

The fourth sentence is Ⓠ Ⓡ Ⓢ Ⓣ Ⓤ

The fifth sentence is Ⓠ Ⓡ Ⓢ Ⓣ Ⓤ

The sixth sentence is Ⓠ Ⓡ Ⓢ Ⓣ Ⓤ

Logical Reasoning

3. Ⓐ Ⓑ Ⓒ Ⓓ Ⓔ

4. Ⓕ Ⓖ Ⓗ Ⓙ Ⓚ

5. Ⓐ Ⓑ Ⓒ Ⓓ Ⓔ

Reading

6. Ⓕ Ⓖ Ⓗ Ⓙ Ⓚ

7. Ⓐ Ⓑ Ⓒ Ⓓ Ⓔ

8. Ⓕ Ⓖ Ⓗ Ⓙ Ⓚ

9. Ⓐ Ⓑ Ⓒ Ⓓ Ⓔ

10. Ⓕ Ⓖ Ⓗ Ⓙ Ⓚ

11. Ⓐ Ⓑ Ⓒ Ⓓ Ⓔ

12. Ⓕ Ⓖ Ⓗ Ⓙ Ⓚ

13. Ⓐ Ⓑ Ⓒ Ⓓ Ⓔ

PART II: MATHEMATICS
PROBLEM SOLVING

14. Ⓕ Ⓖ Ⓗ Ⓙ Ⓚ

15. Ⓐ Ⓑ Ⓒ Ⓓ Ⓔ

16. Ⓕ Ⓖ Ⓗ Ⓙ Ⓚ

17. Ⓐ Ⓑ Ⓒ Ⓓ Ⓔ

18. Ⓕ Ⓖ Ⓗ Ⓙ Ⓚ

19. Ⓐ Ⓑ Ⓒ Ⓓ Ⓔ

20. Ⓕ Ⓖ Ⓗ Ⓙ Ⓚ

21. Ⓐ Ⓑ Ⓒ Ⓓ Ⓔ

22. Ⓕ Ⓖ Ⓗ Ⓙ Ⓚ

23. Ⓐ Ⓑ Ⓒ Ⓓ Ⓔ

24. Ⓕ Ⓖ Ⓗ Ⓙ Ⓚ

25. Ⓐ Ⓑ Ⓒ Ⓓ Ⓔ

26. Ⓕ Ⓖ Ⓗ Ⓙ Ⓚ

answer sheet

Practice Test 5

PART 1: VERBAL

13 Questions • 20 Minutes

QUESTIONS 1–2: SCRAMBLED PARAGRAPHS

Directions: The paragraph below consists of six sentences in scrambled order. The first, or topic, sentence is given, and you are to arrange the rest in an order that makes sense, each sentence following from the one before in that it explains the earlier one or adds to it.

Write the numbers to the left of the letters (in pencil so you can change them as often as you need). When you are satisfied, mark your choices on the answer sheet.

Because you get no partial credit for having only some of the sentences in a paragraph in order and because trying different arrangements to find which reads best requires more time than other test questions, each of the scrambled paragraphs carries twice the weight of other questions on the test.

1. We have all heard of plea bargaining, or "copping a plea," for criminal defendants, but perhaps we are confused about just what it entails.

_____**Q.** Supporters of this system argue that it allows the district attorney to more accurately tailor the punishment to the crime, possibly because the confession itself indicates remorse deserving of consideration.

_____**R.** In return for this favor, the prosecutor will recommend a lighter sentence than the defendant would receive if found guilty by the court.

_____**S.** And still worse to many is that serious criminals are getting off too lightly in courts that value efficiency over justice.

_____**T.** To lighten the caseload handled by busy courts, the prosecutor offers the defense attorney an opportunity to plead guilty to a lesser charge rather than take the case to trial.

_____**U.** Opponents of plea bargaining, on the other hand, believe the defendant is thereby deprived of his constitutional right to a fair trial or her that an innocent person, fearing an unfair outcome at trial, might plead guilty to a crime he or she did not commit.

The second sentence is   Ⓠ Ⓡ Ⓢ Ⓣ Ⓤ

The third sentence is   Ⓠ Ⓡ Ⓢ Ⓣ Ⓤ

The fourth sentence is   Ⓠ Ⓡ Ⓢ Ⓣ Ⓤ

The fifth sentence is   Ⓠ Ⓡ Ⓢ Ⓣ Ⓤ

The sixth sentence is   Ⓠ Ⓡ Ⓢ Ⓣ Ⓤ

2. Recent studies indicate that a commonly accepted principle known as the *contrast effect* works in the sphere of person-to-person attraction.

_____**Q.** For example, presented with two pots of different weights, lifting the lighter one first makes the other seem heavier than it actually is or would seem if lifted first.

_____**R.** This effect influences our evaluations not only to strangers, but also to our close friends and family members, particularly when we see them exposed to someone new for the first time.

_____**S.** In the same way, if there is a beautiful girl at a party and a merely attractive one joins her, that second one will seem almost homely by contrast.

_____**T.** According to the principle, the difference between any two objects is exaggerated by the order in which they are presented.

_____**U.** And it commonly distorts our view of our own attractiveness and abilities.

The second sentence is   Ⓠ Ⓡ Ⓢ Ⓣ Ⓤ

The third sentence is   Ⓠ Ⓡ Ⓢ Ⓣ Ⓤ

The fourth sentence is   Ⓠ Ⓡ Ⓢ Ⓣ Ⓤ

The fifth sentence is   Ⓠ Ⓡ Ⓢ Ⓣ Ⓤ

The sixth sentence is   Ⓠ Ⓡ Ⓢ Ⓣ Ⓤ

QUESTIONS 3–5: LOGICAL REASONING

Directions: Read each question very carefully and choose the **best** answer from the five choices given. Select your answer based **only** on the information provided.

3. Sib is the mother of Reg, and Mos is the brother of Sib. Mos is Reg's

   A. brother.

   B. sister.

   C. aunt.

   D. uncle.

   E. cousin.

4. All rats are animals. All animals have eyes. Some animals have red eyes. Which of the following is always true according to the above information?

   F. Some rats have red eyes.

   G. No rats have red eyes.

   H. All rats have red eyes.

   J. All rats have eyes.

   K. Only animals have red eyes.

The problem below uses a code where one specific letter stands for a word and only that word. The letter representing a word usually is not located directly above the word it represents. Each line of letters stands for the words in the line below.

| (1) V | R | N | P | Q | means |
| At | seven | Kim | eats | dinner. | |

| (2) N | V | R | U | W | means |
| Kim | dines | Fridays | at | seven. | |

| (3) G | Q | T | S | P | means |
| Mondays | Ralph | eats | dinner | alone. | |

| (4) X | R | Q | V | P | means |
| Kim | eats | dinner | at | six. | |

5. What would be the code for the fraction 5/X over seven?

   A. N/Q

   B. R/X

   C. N/X

   D. Q/N

   E. X/N

QUESTIONS 6–13: READING PASSAGES

Directions: Read each passage below and answer the questions that follow. Remember to **use only the information you have read in the passage** when answering the questions; you may reread the passage if necessary.

The presence in our world and over it of what are called Unidentified Flying Objects (UFOs) has been reported for at least fifty years semi-officially, and
5 probably from the beginning of time, for all we know.

Although the records of these sightings are shrouded in secrecy, The Freedom of Information Act (F.I.A.)
10 has permitted "ufologists," including one named Robert Hastings, to obtain copies of some of them from a number of governmental bureaus: the FBI, the National Security Office, the White
15 House, and the CIA, among others. He claims he would have gotten all of them, but to do so, you need to know what each document is called and where it is filed. Browsing is out.

20 The very agencies whose files bulge with reports of individual sightings, group sightings, downed aircraft, and even dogfights with military pilots in the air deny the existence of UFOs and
25 alien tourists. They dismiss reports of sightings as the ravings of maniacs or paranoid personalities, or as having a simple explanation: anything from light reflected from clouds, flattened
30 hailstones, meteors, domestic or foreign aircraft to marsh gases.

Robert Hastings claims that most UFO activity in America has centered around nuclear installations, power
35 stations, and military bases. He even connects UFOs spotted by military radar over Eastern cities with the power blackout of 1966.

The *Star*, a supermarket tabloid not
40 known for verification of its stories, once
claimed that the Soviet government,
under Stalin, kept a Blue Book of 954
case histories of alien visits, including a
secret fifteen-day assignation with Harry
45 Truman in 1945. They also claimed that
Hitler and his henchmen nearly suc-
ceeded in lining up alien assistance in
the war against the allies.

Separating the truth from fiction
50 about UFOs promises to provide enter-
tainment for a long time to come, no
doubt. Perhaps rumors that the reason
for official secrecy is that we aren't ready
to hear about it are part of the truth.

6. What is the overall theme of this passage?

F. People who think there are UFOs
are paranoid.

G. It is hard to know from what we
hear and read if UFO sightings are
real or imaginary.

H. Some people have seen Martians.

J. UFO sightings by world leaders
are convincingly documented and
reported in newspapers.

K. Flying saucers are caused by marsh
gases.

7. We suspect UFOs exist because

A. there have been electrical blackouts.

B. Robert Hastings has had visual
contact with them.

C. there have been so many reports
kept in official files, even though
they are mostly secret.

D. the government keeps secrets about
important matters.

E. we have spiritual need for them.

8. Which of the following are offered as official explanations for UFO sightings?

F. Airplanes from Mars

G. Flattened hailstones, meteors,
marsh gases

H. Secret missions

J. Sightings are reported from mental
institutions.

K. There have been no sightings.

9. We have little reason to believe the Soviet
Blue Book reports of sightings are real
because

A. Mr. Hastings has not seen the Blue
Book.

B. there are no UFOs according to our
government's secret reports.

C. no alien visits have ever been
reported.

D. the *Star's* stories are seldom
verified.

E. we should not question authorities.

The Trois Vallées ski area in France,
site of the 1992 Winter Olympics, bills
itself as the most extensive ski area
in the world. Nine separate towns are
5 linked by a massive network of lifts,
190 in all. They include the world's two
biggest aerial trams (which hold about
sixty people at a time), chair lifts and
gondolas, as well as poma-lifts unique
10 to the Alps, which take a skier up, and
sometimes down, around corners and up
again, along the top of the world.

There are over three hundred miles
of downhill trails, plus all the skiable
15 whiteness between these "pistes," as
trails are called. Amazingly, snowcats,
sixty of them, called "engins de damage"
groom all but the steepest and most
bump-filled of the pistes.

20 Unfortunately, however, the vast
Alpine stretches are losing much of
their old charm, due to overdevelopment
copied from the U.S. As our ski areas each
summer throw up new condominiums or

25 townhouses—many in imitation Alpine
style—European resorts build not merely
a few high-rise vacation homes, but whole
towns that look like cities dropped into
the snow from another planet.

30   Once-homey restaurants in winter
villages have turned into our Amer-
ican-style base lodges serving bad,
and expensive, American fast food. In
addition, the over development has led

35 to enough smog so that from the upper
reaches of the mountains the town below
looks like nothing so much as a bowl of
gray soup.

10. Besides painting a picture of the ski area,
the passage

    F. describes the unfortunate
Americanization of the area.

    G. tells the history of the Trois Vallées.

    H. gives facts about and prices of
European skiing.

    J. describes the best restaurants.

    K. is a typical travelogue.

11. This passage criticizes

    A. skiing in Europe.

    B. engins de damage.

    C. people who ski.

    D. the result of overdevelopment.

    E. the ski-lift system.

12. One can infer from the passage that the
writer is

    F. a young American skier.

    G. a bored traveler.

    H. in favor of all things American.

    J. a longtime skier.

    K. a beginner skier.

13. The "pistes" of the Trois Vallées

    A. are all entirely groomed.

    B. are easy to ski.

    C. have gondolas on them.

    D. cover three hundred miles, most of
them kept groomed.

    E. are better than those in
Switzerland.

PART II: MATHEMATICS
13 Questions • 20 Minutes

The following information is provided for your reference. It will likely not appear in the actual test booklet. You should memorize these formulas and symbols.

FORMULAS

- Area of a circle (with radius r) = πr^2

- Circumference of a circle = $2\pi r$

- Area of a parallelogram (with base b and height h) = bh

- Area of a trapezoid (with parallel sides a and b and height h) = $\frac{1}{2}(a+b)h$

- Volume of a cone or pyramid (with base area b and height h) = $\frac{1}{3}bh$

- Volume of a cylinder (with base area b and height h) = bh

- Volume of a sphere (with radius r) = $\frac{4}{3}\pi r^3$

- Sum of the measures of the angles of a triangle = $180°$

- Area of a triangle:

  Area = $\frac{bh}{2}$
  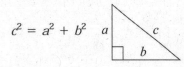

- For a right triangle:

  $c^2 = a^2 + b^2$

DEFINITIONS OF SYMBOLS

= is equal to

≠ is unequal to

< is less than

> is greater than

≤ is less than or equal to

≥ is greater than or equal to

⊥ is perpendicular to

‖ is parallel to

∠ angle

∟ right angle

⇉ parallel lines

NOTES

- Figures may not be drawn to scale. Do not assume any relationship in a diagram unless it is specifically stated or can be figured out from given information.

- Assume that a diagram is in one plane unless the problem specifically states that it is not.

- Reduce all fractions to lowest terms.

QUESTIONS 14–26: PROBLEM SOLVING

Directions: For each question, solve the problem and select the best answer from the choices given.

14. Which fraction has the greatest value?

    F. $\dfrac{3}{4}$

    G. $\dfrac{5}{6}$

    H. $\dfrac{8}{9}$

    J. $\dfrac{5}{8}$

    K. $\dfrac{4}{7}$

15. Which of the following is an irrational number?

    A. $\dfrac{5}{12}$

    B. $33\dfrac{1}{3}\%$

    C. $12\dfrac{1}{2}\%$

    D. $\dfrac{10}{7}$

    E. $\sqrt{26}$

16. For what value of x is $2x + 3 = 3(x + 4)$?

    F. 2

    G. 3

    H. –1

    J. –9

    K. 0

17. The diameter of a circle whose circumference is 47.10 inches is: (use $\pi = 3.14$)

    A. $7\dfrac{1}{2}$ inches

    B. 15.7 inches

    C. 25 inches

    D. 14 inches

    E. 15 inches

18. The least common multiple of 2, 3, 4, and 6 is

    F. 24

    G. 48

    H. 12

    J. 8

    K. 4

19. Square I has area 49 square inches. If each side of square II is 3 times as long as each side of square I, then what is the perimeter of square II?

    A. 28 inches

    B. 12 inches

    C. 84 inches

    D. 147 inches

    E. Cannot be determined

20. Toby drove her car at an average speed of 220 kilometers per hour for $3\dfrac{1}{2}$ hours. How far did she travel?

    F. 220 km

    G. 770 km

    H. 660 km

    J. $3\dfrac{1}{2}$ km

    K. 63 km

21. What is the next number in the sequence 0, 0, 1, 3, 6, 10, _____?

    A. 15

    B. 14

    C. 13

    D. 4

    E. 5

22. If $\dfrac{4}{7}$ of a quantity is 24, then $\dfrac{5}{6}$ of the same quantity is

F. 10

G. 14

H. 28

J. 35

K. 30

23. If $\dfrac{9}{20}$ lies halfway between $\dfrac{2}{5}$ and x, then $x =$

A. $\dfrac{1}{2}$

B. $\dfrac{3}{5}$

C. $\dfrac{3}{7}$

D. $\dfrac{4}{5}$

E. $\dfrac{3}{4}$

24.

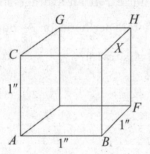

The distance from A to X is

F. 2 inches

G. $\sqrt{3}$ inches

H. $\sqrt{2}$ inches

J. 1 inch

K. $\dfrac{1}{\sqrt{2}}$ inch

25. A motorist travels 120 miles to his destination at an average speed of 60 miles per hour and returns to the starting point at an average speed of 40 miles per hour. His average speed for the entire trip is

A. 53 miles per hour.

B. 52 miles per hour.

C. 50 miles per hour.

D. 48 miles per hour.

E. 45 miles per hour.

26. A snapshot measures $2\dfrac{1}{2}$ inches by $1\dfrac{7}{8}$ inches. It is to be enlarged so that the longer dimension will be 4 inches. The length of the enlarged shorter dimension will be

F. $2\dfrac{1}{2}$ inches.

G. $2\dfrac{5}{8}$ inches.

H. 3 inches.

J. $3\dfrac{3}{8}$ inches.

K. $3\dfrac{5}{8}$ inches.

ANSWER KEY AND EXPLANATIONS

1. TRQUS	7. C	12. J	17. E	22. J
2. TQSRU	8. G	13. D	18. H	23. A
3. D	9. D	14. H	19. C	24. H
4. J	10. F	15. E	20. G	25. D
5. E	11. D	16. J	21. A	26. H
6. G				

PART I: VERBAL
SCRAMBLED PARAGRAPHS

1. **The correct order is TRQUS.** T is the second sentence because it defines plea bargaining from the topic sentence. R is third because it continues the definition from the second sentence. Q is fourth because it gives the reason for plea bargaining. U is fifth because the sentence above starts with "supporters" and this sentence with "opponents," completing the pros and cons. S is sixth because "still worse" has to follow something bad, as in the previous sentence.

2. **The correct order is TQSRU.** T is the second sentence because it describes the principle introduced in the topic sentence. Q is third because it starts with "for example," which does not work after any of the other sentences. S is fourth because "in the same way" refers to the pot example in the third sentence and connects to the person-to-person attraction mentioned in the topic sentence. R is fifth because it refers back to strangers, which could be the two girls at the party. U is sixth because it finishes the "person-to-person" connection.

LOGICAL REASONING

3. **The correct answer is D.** First show Sib as Reg's mother. Next show Mos as Sib's brother. Now it should be apparent that Mos is Reg's uncle.

Sib (mother) ——— Mos (brother of Sib)
|
Reg (child)

4. **The correct answer is J.** Use circles of domains to solve these "all, some" problems:

   1. All rats are animals = The domain of rats fits into the domain of animals.

   2. All animals have eyes = The domain of animals fits into the domain of eyes.

   3. Some animals have red eyes = The domain of red eyes fits inside the animal domain:

   Separate from rats F   Totally encompassing rats J

   Partly intersecting rats G   Totally inside rats H   The same domain as rats K

   All answers 4F—4K above *could* be true, but the only one that is *always* true is 4J.

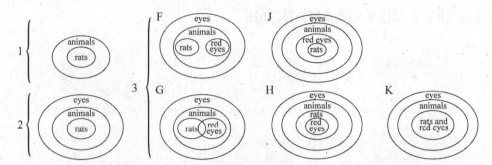

5. **The correct answer is E.** The question deals with the letter codes for six and seven. After reading the sentences it is apparent that the word six appears only in sentence 4. By checking each letter above sentence 4, every letter except X appears in other sentences as well as sentence 4. Therefore, X must stand for six. By finding that the word seven appears only in sentences 1 and 2 you must find a letter that only appears in sentences 1 and 2. V and R appear in sentences 1, 2, and 4, P appears in sentences 1, 3, and 4; Q appears in sentences 1, 3, and 4. That leaves N which appears in only sentences 1 and 2. Therefore, N must stand for seven. The answer six over seven is thus X/N.

READING PASSAGES

6. **The correct answer is G.** The passage deals with whether UFOs are real or nonexistent by reviewing some of the pros and cons on the subject, but does not provide a definitive answer. Choices F, H, and J contain false statements besides not being the main idea of the passage. Choice K is only part of what the passage is concerned with.

7. **The correct answer is C.** Choice C is correct because we have learned that so many government agencies have files on UFOs. Choice D may sound similar, but the mere existence of government secrets has nothing to do with UFOs. Choice A. may be important to Hastings, but doesn't make others suspect UFOs. Choices B and E are meaningless.

8. **The correct answer is G.** It is mentioned in paragraph three that natural phenomena such as meteors, hailstones, and marsh gases are mistakenly identified as UFOs. None of the other choices are found in the passage except choice K, which is a misstatement.

9. **The correct answer is D.** Since the report was in the *Star*, which is a very questionable source, we cannot assume that the report is true.

10. **The correct answer is F.** Choice K is a possibility, but the typical travelogue tells more of the good and less of the bad. Choices G, H, and J are wrong because there is nothing of these subjects in the passage. Choice F is correct.

11. **The correct answer is D.** The only criticism in this passage is of choice D, the overdevelopment. The other options are mentioned but surely not criticized.

12. **The correct answer is J.** You might guess the writer to be either young or bored, or even a beginner, but nothing in the passage backs it up. The author obviously objects to some things American (overdevelopment of ski areas, for instance) so choice H is wrong. You should definitely get the feeling the writer is neither a new skier, nor even new to European skiing, because he/she knows how things once were there. Hence, choice J is right.

13. **The correct answer is D.** Choice A is wrong because the passage says that the steepest and bumpiest trails are not groomed, and we can assume choice B is wrong if there are ungroomed steep and bumpy trails. Choice C is wrong because gondolas are not on the trails, but above, which you may not know except that one kind is said to go up and down and around corners, while trails all go down. Choice E is wrong because there is no mention of Switzerland. Choice D is correct as stated in the second paragraph.

Part II: Mathematics

PROBLEM SOLVING

14. The correct answer is H.

$$\frac{3}{4} = .75$$

$$\frac{5}{6} = .83\bar{3}$$

$$\frac{8}{9} = .8\bar{8}$$

$$\frac{5}{8} = .625$$

$$\frac{6}{7} = .857$$

15. The correct answer is E. A rational number is any number that may be written as a fraction with the denominator *not* equal to zero (i.e., $1 = \frac{1}{1}$, $2 = \frac{2}{1}$, $\frac{3}{4}$). Therefore, $\frac{5}{12}$ and $\frac{10}{7}$ are automatically rational. $33\frac{1}{3}\% = \frac{1}{3}$ and $12\frac{1}{2}\% = \frac{1}{8}$, so all are rational except $\sqrt{26}$, which is a non-terminating, non-repeating decimal.

16. The correct answer is J.

$$2x + 3 = 3(x + 4)$$
$$2x + 3 = 3x + 12$$
$$3 = x + 12$$
$$-9 = x$$

17. The correct answer is E. The formula for circumference = $\pi \times d$ (same as $2\pi r$). Therefore, $C = \pi d$; C = 47.10 inches; $\pi = 3.14$.

$$47.10 = 3.14d \quad (\text{now divide both sides by } 3.14)$$

$$\frac{47.10}{3.14} = \frac{3.14d}{3.14}$$

$$15 = d$$

$$\begin{array}{r} 15 \\ 3.14\overline{)47.10} \\ \underline{31\,4} \\ 15\,70 \\ 15\,70 \end{array}$$

18. The correct answer is H. 12 is the least common multiple of 2, 3, 4, and 6.

19. The correct answer is C. In square I, $x^2 = 49$, so $x = 7$. Thus, each side of square II is 21, and the perimeter of square II is 21 + 21 + 21 + 21 = 84.

20. The correct answer is G. Rate × Time = Distance

$$220 \times 3\frac{1}{2} = 770 \, \text{km}$$

21. The correct answer is A.

0   0   1   3   6   10   15 is the next number.

+0 +1 +2 +3 +4   +5

22. The correct answer is J. Let x = quantity $\frac{4}{7}x = 24$

$$\left(\frac{7}{4}\right)\frac{4}{7}x = 24\left(\frac{7}{4}\right)$$

$$x = 42$$

$$\frac{5}{6} \times \overset{7}{\cancel{42}} = 35$$

23. The correct answer is A. If $\frac{9}{20}$ lies halfway between $\frac{2}{5}$ and x, then $\frac{9}{20}$ is the average

of $\frac{2}{5}$ and x.

$$\frac{\frac{2}{5}+x}{2} = \frac{9}{20}$$

$$\frac{2}{5}+x = \frac{18}{20}$$

$$\frac{2}{5}+x = \frac{9}{10}$$

$$x = \frac{9}{10} - \frac{2}{5} = \frac{9}{10} - \frac{4}{10}$$

$$x = \frac{5}{10} = \frac{1}{2}$$

24. The correct answer is H. The face of the cube is a square, 1" by 1". Use the Pythagorean theorem to find the length of the diagonal of the square.

$$c^2 = a^2 + b^2$$
$$c^2 = 1^2 + 1^2$$
$$c^2 = 2$$
$$c = \sqrt{2}$$

25. The correct answer is D. The average speed for the entire trip is the total distance (240 miles) divided by the total time (5 hours), which yields 48 mph.

26. The correct answer is H. This is a proportion problem. Set up the proportion as follows:

$$\frac{2\frac{1}{2}}{4} = \frac{1\frac{7}{8}}{?}$$

Substitute x for $?$: $\quad \dfrac{2\frac{1}{2}}{4} = \dfrac{1\frac{7}{8}}{x}$

Cross-multiply: $\quad \dfrac{2\frac{1}{2}}{4} \bowtie \dfrac{1\frac{7}{8}}{x}$

$$2\frac{1}{2}x = 4 \cdot 1\frac{7}{8}$$

Divide both sides by the coefficient of x and calculate:

$$\frac{5}{2}x = \frac{60}{8}$$

$$x = \frac{60}{8} \div \frac{5}{2}$$

$$x = \frac{60}{8} \times \frac{2}{5}$$

$$x = 3$$

ANSWER SHEET PRACTICE TEST 6
Part I: Verbal

Scrambled Paragraphs

Paragraph 1

The second sentence is Ⓠ Ⓡ Ⓢ Ⓣ Ⓤ

The third sentence is Ⓠ Ⓡ Ⓢ Ⓣ Ⓤ

The fourth sentence is Ⓠ Ⓡ Ⓢ Ⓣ Ⓤ

The fifth sentence is Ⓠ Ⓡ Ⓢ Ⓣ Ⓤ

The sixth sentence is Ⓠ Ⓡ Ⓢ Ⓣ Ⓤ

Paragraph 2

The second sentence is Ⓠ Ⓡ Ⓢ Ⓣ Ⓤ

The third sentence is Ⓠ Ⓡ Ⓢ Ⓣ Ⓤ

The fourth sentence is Ⓠ Ⓡ Ⓢ Ⓣ Ⓤ

The fifth sentence is Ⓠ Ⓡ Ⓢ Ⓣ Ⓤ

The sixth sentence is Ⓠ Ⓡ Ⓢ Ⓣ Ⓤ

Logical Reasoning

3. Ⓐ Ⓑ Ⓒ Ⓓ Ⓔ

4. Ⓕ Ⓖ Ⓗ Ⓙ Ⓚ

5. Ⓐ Ⓑ Ⓒ Ⓓ Ⓔ

Reading

6. Ⓕ Ⓖ Ⓗ Ⓙ Ⓚ

7. Ⓐ Ⓑ Ⓒ Ⓓ Ⓔ

8. Ⓕ Ⓖ Ⓗ Ⓙ Ⓚ

9. Ⓐ Ⓑ Ⓒ Ⓓ Ⓔ

10. Ⓕ Ⓖ Ⓗ Ⓙ Ⓚ

11. Ⓐ Ⓑ Ⓒ Ⓓ Ⓔ

12. Ⓕ Ⓖ Ⓗ Ⓙ Ⓚ

13. Ⓐ Ⓑ Ⓒ Ⓓ Ⓔ

PART II: MATHEMATICS
PROBLEM SOLVING

14. Ⓕ Ⓖ Ⓗ Ⓙ Ⓚ

15. Ⓐ Ⓑ Ⓒ Ⓓ Ⓔ

16. Ⓕ Ⓖ Ⓗ Ⓙ Ⓚ

17. Ⓐ Ⓑ Ⓒ Ⓓ Ⓔ

18. Ⓕ Ⓖ Ⓗ Ⓙ Ⓚ

19. Ⓐ Ⓑ Ⓒ Ⓓ Ⓔ

20. Ⓕ Ⓖ Ⓗ Ⓙ Ⓚ

21. Ⓐ Ⓑ Ⓒ Ⓓ Ⓔ

22. Ⓕ Ⓖ Ⓗ Ⓙ Ⓚ

23. Ⓐ Ⓑ Ⓒ Ⓓ Ⓔ

24. Ⓕ Ⓖ Ⓗ Ⓙ Ⓚ

25. Ⓐ Ⓑ Ⓒ Ⓓ Ⓔ

26. Ⓕ Ⓖ Ⓗ Ⓙ Ⓚ

answer sheet

Practice Test 6

PART 1: VERBAL

13 Questions • 20 Minutes

QUESTIONS 1–2: SCRAMBLED PARAGRAPHS

Directions: The paragraph below consists of six sentences in scrambled order. The first, or topic, sentence is given, and you are to arrange the rest in an order that makes sense, each sentence following from the one before in that it explains the earlier one or adds to it.

Write the numbers to the left of the letters (in pencil so you can change them as often as you need). When you are satisfied, mark your choices on the answer sheet.

Because you get no partial credit for having only some of the sentences in a paragraph in order and because trying different arrangements to find which reads best requires more time than other test questions, each of the scrambled paragraphs carries twice the weight of other questions on the test.

1. A belief—or, more accurately, superstition—accepted worldwide is that a fresh chicken egg will balance on its broad end only on the first day of spring.

_____**Q.** It seems to have started in ancient China, where oddly enough, the first day of spring is sometime in February, long ahead of the vernal equinox.

_____**R.** Strangely enough, the superstition not only persists, but also occasionally bears itself out: some eggs do balance (although most do not).

_____**S.** Why not experiment for yourself, trying this trick in February like the ancient Chinese and again on the first day of spring in March for a few years in a row, making sure to keep track of your success record!

_____**T.** Convincing explanations for the occasional success include the motivation of strong belief or the possibility that the standing egg has been placed on a rough surface, such as concrete.

_____**U.** A less-convincing explanation is that there are special gravitational forces resulting from the spring equinox, a notion backed up by no reputable astronomer or physicist.

The second sentence is   Ⓠ Ⓡ Ⓢ Ⓣ Ⓤ

The third sentence is   Ⓠ Ⓡ Ⓢ Ⓣ Ⓤ

The fourth sentence is   Ⓠ Ⓡ Ⓢ Ⓣ Ⓤ

The fifth sentence is   Ⓠ Ⓡ Ⓢ Ⓣ Ⓤ

The sixth sentence is   Ⓠ Ⓡ Ⓢ Ⓣ Ⓤ

2. You may have seen on a city street a bearded man carrying a sign announcing the imminent end of the world—any city, any street, one of many men.

_____**Q.** That man may be merely paranoid, but predicting the end of the world has been a favorite pastime of religious groups and serious thinkers alike.

_____**R.** When the club's prediction failed to materialize by 1990, its members cleverly took credit, claiming that by alerting the world to the dangers, it had led us to wiser uses of our waning resources.

_____**S.** In 1975, Nobel Prize winner George Wald predicted the end for 1985, and popular writers Paul and Anne Ehrlich in their 1968 book _Population Explosion, Population Bomb_ predicted that we would all starve to death soon.

_____**T.** Microbiologist René Dubos, another respected scientist, in 1972, cited overindustrialization as the likely cause of the world's demise by 1997.

_____**U.** At about the same time, the Club of Rome predicted the end by the 1980s due to the shortage of energy, raw materials, and minerals in an overpopulated world.

The second sentence is   Ⓠ Ⓡ Ⓢ Ⓣ Ⓤ
The third sentence is   Ⓠ Ⓡ Ⓢ Ⓣ Ⓤ
The fourth sentence is   Ⓠ Ⓡ Ⓢ Ⓣ Ⓤ
The fifth sentence is   Ⓠ Ⓡ Ⓢ Ⓣ Ⓤ
The sixth sentence is   Ⓠ Ⓡ Ⓢ Ⓣ Ⓤ

QUESTIONS 3–5: LOGICAL REASONING

Directions: Read each question very carefully and choose the **best** answer from the five choices given. Select your answer based **only** on the information provided.

3. On the planet of Orgo, there are only liars and truthtellers. You send a radio message in the Orgonian language, and it is picked up by an Orgonian radio operator, who sends you back an answer. The message you send is: "Can you understand this message, and are you telling the truth?"

Of the following answers, which one is definitely sent by an Orgonian liar?

A. no, no

B. yes, yes

C. no, yes

D. yes, no

E. No answer is possible with the given information

4. Suppose you have a big map of the world, and a fly is standing on New York state. It walks northwest in a straight line and stops on Michigan. It then walks due North to the North Pole. It then walks directly to a point in California southwest of Michigan. The fly then walks due East back to New York.

Draw a figure made by the fly's walk. Count the number of interior angles. Then subtract the number of angles under 90°. How many angles are left?

F. 0

G. 1

H. 2

J. 3

K. 4

In the code below each letter stands for a word and only that word. The letter standing for a word may or may not be placed directly over the word it stands for. Each line of letters stands for the words in the line below.

(1) R   Z   N   M   L   means

     Bob   likes   Maria   and   Ashan.

(2) Q   M   R   P   O   means

     Stu   and   Bob   are   friends.

(3) T   Z   S   M   L   means

     Jill   likes   Stephanie   and   Ashan.

(4) L   Z   M   O   X   means

     Ashana   likes   and   enjoys   friends.

5. In sentence 4, which letter is *definitely* above the word it stands for?

A. M

B. Z

C. L

D. X

E. O

QUESTIONS 6–13: READING PASSAGES

Directions: Read each passage below and answer the questions that follow. Remember to **use only the information you have read in the passage** when answering the questions; you may reread the passage if necessary.

Expert health researchers consider smoking the single most harmful thing a person can do to him- or herself. Smoking, they have established, increases the risk
5 of early mortality or disability, not only from lung cancer and heart disease, but also from cancer of the pancreas, kidney, and bladder.

The number of male smokers in
10 America has declined since 1950 from 69 percent of men to 29 percent, with a corresponding decline in lung cancer among men. It has also been found that it takes fifteen years for a smoker to undo
15 the damage from his habit once he quits.

The downside of the research is the finding that while men were quitting, more women took up smoking, now over 30 percent more, and lung cancer
20 is now the cause of more female deaths than breast cancer, which had been the number one killer of women.

Research also shows that when a person drinks alcohol while smoking
25 cigarettes, the damage is more than twice as great. And most smokers tend to have a cigarette with their cocktail-hour drink.

Research is ongoing, with the U.S. government taking an active position
30 in the fight for a smoke-free society. Laws now forbid cigarette advertising on television and radio and smoking on domestic flights and in theaters. Many restaurants forbid or limit smoking.
35 But despite smokers' and former smokers' growing awareness of tobacco's dangers, young people, who also know better, are still starting in increasing numbers what may be a lifelong, dan-
40 gerous addiction.

6. When alcohol and cigarettes are taken together, they are

   F. worse than when taken apart.

   G. more addictive.

   H. called the cocktail hour.

   J. affecting more women.

   K. somewhat unusual.

7. Which of the following best tells what this passage is mainly about?

   A. The government and tobacco

   B. Banning the killer tobacco

   C. The successes and failures of the battle against smoking

   D. Statistics as the way to success in stopping smoking

   E. Why our society is addicted to drugs and cigarettes

8. According to the passage, smoking is illegal in (on)

   F running marathons.

   G. all places of worship.

   H. domestic flights and theaters.

   J. transcontinental flights.

   K. places where food is consumed.

9. This passage indicates that smoking is on the rise among

   A. women and young people.

   B. white men.

   C. third-world countries.

   D. prison inmates.

   E. the health conscious.

Would it surprise you to know that environmentally aware architects today are examining what we know of "sustainable" design models of the past,
5 even those of thousands of years ago? Sustainable is a word in the lexicon of environmentalists, used to designate development that protects and helps sustain the earth's ecology.
10 Long before the invention of central heating and air conditioning, the early Greeks, Romans, Chinese, and Native Americans, among other civilizations, built their homes with careful regard to
15 wind, water, and sun. Shelter from the wind, access to a source of water, and maximum heat and light from the sun were paramount.

When the Roman Empire suffered a
20 shortage of wood for fuel, "solar access rights" were written into law, and well-placed windows were a sign of wealth and intelligence. "In ancient China," according to the Natural Resources
25 Defense Council, "shamans (magicians) were enlisted to find the most naturally auspicious spots for homes (and graves)." In a Socratic dialogue by the Greek writer Xenophon, in about 400 B.C., the character
30 Isomachus brings his bride back to his solar-oriented home and shows off "living rooms for the family that are cool in the summer and warm in the winter."

Modern civilization slowly unlearned
35 the early lessons, building homes and commercial structures that battle nature, climate, and the elements. Fuel and other resources are wasted through poorly designed and placed buildings. Says S.
40 David Freeman in an environmental journal, "Americans expect—indeed they insist upon—sufficient energy to maintain the temperature they desire in every inch of indoor living and working
45 space no matter how hot or cold it may be outdoors. The typical American building is now too hot in the winter and too cold in the summer."

An average house in our suburbs uses
50 as much energy as an entire country town one hundred years ago, where houses were built with southern exposures and had fewer and smaller windows to minimize heat loss. There were more
55 trees to provide summer shade, without filtering winter sun.

It is hoped that tomorrow's builders will have taken a judicious look at yesterday's.

10. A good title for this passage would be:

   F. Modern Energy Consumption

   G. The History of Architecture

   H. Learning Energy Conservation from History

   J. The Ancient World

   K. Waste in Building

11. The early Romans

   A. styled their houses after the Chinese.

   B. were technologically advanced compared to now.

   C. applied Greek techniques in their homes.

   D. built environmentally sound homes.

   E. were sun worshipers.

12. Sustainable designs in architecture

   F. are economically unfeasible.

   G. conserve energy.

   H. use no insulation.

   J. are modern ideas.

   K. are typical in the U.S.

13. The passage suggests that Americans today

   A. should stop living in suburbs.

   B. should retain all the trees.

   C. depend more on air conditioning.

   D. should accept cooler indoor temperatures in winter.

   E. All of the above

PART II: MATHEMATICS
13 Questions • 20 Minutes

The following information is provided for your reference. It will likely not appear in the actual test booklet. You should memorize these formulas and symbols.

FORMULAS

- Area of a circle (with radius r) = πr^2

- Circumference of a circle = $2\pi r$

- Area of a parallelogram (with base b and height h) = bh

- Area of a trapezoid (with parallel sides a and b and height h) = $\frac{1}{2}(a+b)h$

- Volume of a cone or pyramid (with base area b and height h) = $\frac{1}{3}bh$

- Volume of a cylinder (with base area b and height h) = bh

- Volume of a sphere $\left(\text{with radius } r\right)$ = $\frac{4}{3}\pi r^3$

- Sum of the measures of the angles of a triangle = $180°$

- Area of a triangle:

  Area = $\frac{bh}{2}$

- For a right triangle:

  $c^2 = a^2 + b^2$

DEFINITIONS OF SYMBOLS

$=$ is equal to

$\neq$ is unequal to

$<$ is less than

$>$ is greater than

$\leq$ is less than or equal to

$\geq$ is greater than or equal to

$\perp$ is perpendicular to

$\parallel$ is parallel to

$\angle$ angle

$\llcorner$ right angle

$\rightrightarrows$ parallel lines

NOTES

- Figures may not be drawn to scale. Do not assume any relationship in a diagram unless it is specifically stated or can be figured out from given information.

- Assume that a diagram is in one plane unless the problem specifically states that it is not.

- Reduce all fractions to lowest terms.

QUESTIONS 14–26: PROBLEM SOLVING

Directions: For each question, solve the problem and select the best answer from the choices given.

14. The union of (1, 2, 3), (3, 4, 5), and (1, 3, 5) is

    F. (1, 3, 5)

    G. (1, 2, 3, 4, 5)

    H. (3, 4, 5)

    J. (2, 4)

    K. an empty set.

15. In the following table, what must you do to make the numbers in the x-row the same as the numbers in the y-row?

x	2	3	4	5
y	6	8	10	12

    A. Multiply by 3

    B. Divide by 3

    C. Multiply by 3 and subtract 1

    D. Multiply by 2 and add 2

    E. Add 4

16. A man walks from point A to point B to point C. If it takes 1 hour to walk the 3 miles from A to B, and 3 hours to walk the 6 miles from B to C, what is his average speed for the whole trip A—B—C?

    F. $\dfrac{1.5 \text{ mi.}}{\text{hr.}}$

    G. $\dfrac{3 \text{ mi.}}{\text{hr.}}$

    H. $\dfrac{2 \text{ mi.}}{\text{hr.}}$

    J. $\dfrac{6 \text{ mi.}}{\text{hr.}}$

    K. $\dfrac{2.25 \text{ mi.}}{\text{hr}}$

17. A plumber has a pipe 18 feet long. He used the following lengths on three separate jobs: $7\frac{1}{2}$ inches, 3 feet, 2 yards. How big was the piece of pipe he had left?

    A. $91\frac{1}{2}$ inches

    B. $112\frac{1}{2}$ inches

    C. 9 feet

    D. 11 feet

    E. $100\frac{1}{2}$ inches

18. Solve for x: $x = 5\left(\dfrac{1}{10} - x\right)$

    F. $\dfrac{1}{5}$

    G. $\dfrac{2}{5}$

    H. 2

    J. $\dfrac{1}{12}$

    K. −2

19. If x dollars will buy y pounds of chopped meat, how many dollars are needed to buy z pounds of the same meat?

    A. $\dfrac{xz}{y}$

    B. xyz

    C. $\dfrac{z}{xy}$

    D. $\dfrac{x + y}{z}$

    E. $\dfrac{xy}{z}$

20. When a number is added to $\frac{1}{3}$ of itself, the result is 16. The number is

F. 12

G. $21\frac{1}{3}$

H. 20

J. $5\frac{1}{3}$

K. 4

21. Find the value of $a \div b + c \times d - e$, if $a = 6$, $b = -3$, $c = 10$, $d = -2$, and $e = 1$.

A. $-\frac{1}{4}$

B. -23

C. $\frac{5}{7}$

D. 24

E. $-\frac{5}{23}$

22. Find the area of the figure shown.

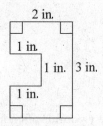

F. 1 sq. in.

G. 5 sq. in.

H. 6 sq. in.

J. 7 sq. in.

K. 12 sq. in.

23. If a man has only quarters and dimes totaling $2.00, the number of dimes can be

A. 2

B. 10

C. 8

D. 6

E. 3

24. From a piece of tin in the shape of a square 6 inches on a side, the largest possible circle is cut out. Of the following, the ratio of the area of the circle to the area of the original square is closest in value to

F. $\frac{4}{5}$

G. $\frac{2}{3}$

H. $\frac{3}{5}$

J. $\frac{7}{9}$

K. $\frac{3}{4}$

25. If the outer diameter of a metal pipe is 2.84 inches and the inner diameter is 1.94 inches, the thickness of the metal is

A. 0.45 in.

B. 0.90 in.

C. 1.42 in.

D. 1.94 in.

E. 2.39 in.

26. A sportswriter claims that her football predictions are accurate 60% of the time. During football season, a fan kept records and found that the writer was inaccurate for a total of 16 games, although she did maintain her 60% accuracy. For how many games was the sportswriter accurate?

F. 5

G. 15

H. 24

J. 40

K. 60

ANSWER KEY AND EXPLANATIONS

1. QRTUS	7. C	12. G	17. E	22. G
2. QSTUR	8. H	13. D	18. J	23. B
3. C	9. A	14. G	19. A	24. J
4. G	10. H	15. D	20. F	25. A
5. A	11. D	16. K	21. B	26. H
6. F				

PART I: VERBAL
SCRAMBLED PARAGRAPHS

1. **The correct order is QRTUS.** Q is the second sentence because it tells where the superstition got its start. R is third because it refers to the persistence of the superstition. T is fourth because it gives explanations for the occasional success mentioned in the previous sentence. U is fifth because as the previous sentence starts with "convincing explanations," this immediately follows with "less convincing explanation." S is sixth because it concludes the paragraph without adding new facts.

2. **The correct order is QSTUR.** Q is the second sentence because it explains why these men behave as described in the topic sentence. S is third because all the examples in this paragraph are roughly chronological, with this being the earliest. T is fourth because it lists a somewhat later example. U is fifth because it is the latest example. R is sixth because it continues the example of the Club of Rome from the previous sentence.

LOGICAL REASONING

3. **The correct answer is C.** A liar must lie. So if he understands the message, he would say he doesn't understand it. And of course he would lie and say that he is telling the truth.

4. **The correct answer is G.** Look at the diagram. 4 is the only angle over 90°.

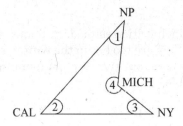

5. **The correct answer is A.** The question directs you to sentence 4. By looking at the letters and checking their appearance in other sentences we find that *Ashana* appears in sentences 1, 2, and 4 and always has L above it. *Likes* appears in sentences 1, 2, and 4 and always has Z above it. But the letters L and Z could be switched over *Ashana* and *likes* and they still would appear in sentences 1, 2, and 4. The letter O appears in sentences 2 and 4 and has a different word below so it's out of the running. X is over *friends* in sentence 4 and O is over friends in sentence 2, so it's out of the running. M, on the other hand, appears in sentences 1, 2, 3, and 4 and always appears above *and* and it's the only word and letter combination that appears in all 4 sentences.

READING PASSAGES

6. **The correct answer is F.** It is possible that alcohol and cigarettes taken together are more addictive since they so often go together, but the passage does not state this. It does say that choice F is correct, and the other choices are all wrong.

7. **The correct answer is C.** This passage does mention what the government is doing about tobacco; it does mention places that ban smoking or cigarette advertising, choices A and B, but choice C is the main thrust of the passage: who is quitting and who is starting. Choices D and E have nothing to do with this passage.

8. **The correct answer is H.** The only places mentioned in the passage where smoking is banned are listed in choice H. Consequently, even though it might actually be true of some of the other possible choices, they are incorrect.

9. **The correct answer is A.** You may have heard that choices C and D are true, but not from this passage, which says only that women and young people are smoking more, choice A. Choices B and E are incorrect.

10. **The correct answer is H.** The passage is all about energy conservation and about how it was accomplished in the past. Choice F might appeal to you, but modern energy consumption is only one aspect of the passage. The other choices, E, J, and K, are too broad.

11. **The correct answer is D.** Paragraphs two and three mention the Romans as building environmentally sound structures. The other answers are incorrect because none of them is stated in this passage.

12. **The correct answer is G.** The passage is about energy waste and conservation in relation to architecture. Choices F, J, and K are the opposite of what is stated; choice H is not stated anywhere in the passage.

13. **The correct answer is D.** The fourth paragraph, which criticizes modern homes and the expectations of those who live in them, states that they are too hot in the winter, suggesting they should be cooler. Choices B and C may be true, but they are not mentioned in the passage. Choices A and E are easily disregardable.

Part II: Mathematics

PROBLEM SOLVING

14. The correct answer is G. The union is the addition of sets. Therefore, (1, 2, 3) + (3, 4, 5) + (1, 3, 5) = (1, 2, 3, 4, 5)

15. The correct answer is D. Multiply by 2 and add 2. In other words, if you double x and add 2, you will produce y.

16. The correct answer is K.

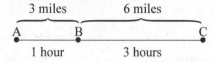

The total distance covered is 9 miles; the total time it takes is 4 hours. Thus, the average speed is

$$\frac{9\text{ miles}}{4\text{ hours}} = \frac{2.25\text{ mi.}}{\text{hr.}}$$

17. The correct answer is E.

1) $7\frac{1}{2}'' = 7\frac{1}{2}''$

$\quad\; 3' = 36''$

$2\,\text{yds} = 72''$

$\overline{\qquad\quad 115\frac{1}{2}''}$

2) $18' = 18 \times 12 = 216''$

3) $216'' - 115\frac{1}{2}'' = 100\frac{1}{2}''$

18. The correct answer is J.

$x = 5\left(\frac{1}{10} - x\right) \qquad 6x = \frac{5}{10} \qquad \frac{6x}{6} = \frac{1}{2} \times \frac{1}{6}$

$x = \frac{5}{10} - 5x \qquad\quad 6x = \frac{1}{2} \qquad\quad x = \frac{1}{12}$

19. The correct answer is A. Set up a proportion:

$$\frac{x\,\text{dollars}}{y\,\text{pounds}} = \frac{?\,\text{dollars}}{z\,\text{pounds}}$$

$$?\,\text{dollars} = \frac{xz}{y}$$

20. The correct answer is F. Let x = the number.

$\frac{1x}{3} = \frac{1}{3}$ of itself

Therefore, $x + \frac{1x}{3} = 16$ or $1\frac{1x}{3} = 16$

$\frac{4}{3x} = 16$ (multiply both sides by $\frac{3}{4}$)

$\left(\frac{3}{4}\right)\frac{4x}{3} = \frac{\overset{4}{\cancel{16}}}{1}\left(\frac{3}{\cancel{4}}\right)$

$\qquad x = 12$

21. The correct answer is B.

$$a \div b + c \times d - e = \frac{a}{b} + cd - e$$
$$= \frac{6}{-3} + (10)(-2) - 1$$
$$= -2 + (-20) - 1$$
$$= -23$$

22. The correct answer is E.

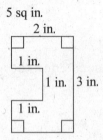

5 sq in.

Area of a rectangle = length × width

2 × 3 = 6 sq. in.

Then subtract the area of the small square: 6 sq. in. – 1 sq. in. = 5 sq. in.

23. The correct answer is B. If a man has only quarters and dimes totaling $2.00, then he must have an even number of quarters, for only if he has an even number of quarters is it possible to add dimes to equal exactly $2.00. If a man has 2 quarters (50¢), he will need 15 dimes ($1.50) to equal $2.00. If he has 4 quarters ($1.00), he will need 10 dimes ($1.00) to equal $2.00. If he has 6 quarters ($1.50), he will need 5 dimes (50¢) to equal $2.00. Only 10 is offered as an answer choice.

24. The correct answer is J. To find the ratio of the circle to the area of the square, first find the area of each. Note that the diameter of the circle equals the width of the square.

Area of the square = 6″ × 6″ = 36 sq. in.

Area of circle = $\pi 3^2 = 9\pi = 9 \cdot \frac{22}{7} = \frac{198}{7} = 28$ sq. in., approximately

Ratio of the area of the circle to the area of the square : $\frac{28}{36} = \frac{7}{9}$

25. The correct answer is A. The difference is 0.90 inch, but the outside diameter consists of two thicknesses of metal (one on each side). Therefore, the thickness of the metal is 0.90 ÷ 2 = 0.45 inch.

26. The correct answer is H. If 60% of the games were predicted accurately, 40% of the games were predicted inaccurately.

Let x = games played

.40x = 16

x = 40 games played

40 – 16 = 24 games won

Therefore, the sportswriter was accurate for 24 games.

ANSWER SHEET PRACTICE TEST 7
Part I: Verbal

Scrambled Paragraphs

Paragraph 1

The second sentence is ⓠ Ⓡ Ⓢ Ⓣ Ⓤ

The third sentence is ⓠ Ⓡ Ⓢ Ⓣ Ⓤ

The fourth sentence is ⓠ Ⓡ Ⓢ Ⓣ Ⓤ

The fifth sentence is ⓠ Ⓡ Ⓢ Ⓣ Ⓤ

The sixth sentence is ⓠ Ⓡ Ⓢ Ⓣ Ⓤ

Paragraph 2

The second sentence is ⓠ Ⓡ Ⓢ Ⓣ Ⓤ

The third sentence is ⓠ Ⓡ Ⓢ Ⓣ Ⓤ

The fourth sentence is ⓠ Ⓡ Ⓢ Ⓣ Ⓤ

The fifth sentence is ⓠ Ⓡ Ⓢ Ⓣ Ⓤ

The sixth sentence is ⓠ Ⓡ Ⓢ Ⓣ Ⓤ

Logical Reasoning

3. Ⓐ Ⓑ Ⓒ Ⓓ Ⓔ

4. Ⓕ Ⓖ Ⓗ Ⓙ Ⓚ

5. Ⓐ Ⓑ Ⓒ Ⓓ Ⓔ

Reading

6. Ⓕ Ⓖ Ⓗ Ⓙ Ⓚ

7. Ⓐ Ⓑ Ⓒ Ⓓ Ⓔ

8. Ⓕ Ⓖ Ⓗ Ⓙ Ⓚ

9. Ⓐ Ⓑ Ⓒ Ⓓ Ⓔ

10. Ⓕ Ⓖ Ⓗ Ⓙ Ⓚ

11. Ⓐ Ⓑ Ⓒ Ⓓ Ⓔ

12. Ⓕ Ⓖ Ⓗ Ⓙ Ⓚ

13. Ⓐ Ⓑ Ⓒ Ⓓ Ⓔ

PART II: MATHEMATICS
PROBLEM SOLVING

14. Ⓕ Ⓖ Ⓗ Ⓙ Ⓚ

15. Ⓐ Ⓑ Ⓒ Ⓓ Ⓔ

16. Ⓕ Ⓖ Ⓗ Ⓙ Ⓚ

17. Ⓐ Ⓑ Ⓒ Ⓓ Ⓔ

18. Ⓕ Ⓖ Ⓗ Ⓙ Ⓚ

19. Ⓐ Ⓑ Ⓒ Ⓓ Ⓔ

20. Ⓕ Ⓖ Ⓗ Ⓙ Ⓚ

21. Ⓐ Ⓑ Ⓒ Ⓓ Ⓔ

22. Ⓕ Ⓖ Ⓗ Ⓙ Ⓚ

23. Ⓐ Ⓑ Ⓒ Ⓓ Ⓔ

24. Ⓕ Ⓖ Ⓗ Ⓙ Ⓚ

25. Ⓐ Ⓑ Ⓒ Ⓓ Ⓔ

26. Ⓕ Ⓖ Ⓗ Ⓙ Ⓚ

answer sheet

Practice Test 7

PART 1: VERBAL

13 Questions • 20 Minutes
QUESTIONS 1–2: SCRAMBLED PARAGRAPHS

Directions: The paragraph below consists of six sentences in scrambled order. The first, or topic, sentence is given, and you are to arrange the rest in an order that makes sense, each sentence following from the one before in that it explains the earlier one or adds to it.

Write the numbers to the left of the letters (in pencil so you can change them as often as you need). When you are satisfied, mark your choices on the answer sheet.

Because you get no partial credit for having only some of the sentences in a paragraph in order and because trying different arrangements to find which reads best requires more time than other test questions, each of the scrambled paragraphs carries twice the weight of other questions on the test.

1. For some reason, the tarantula—an often large, powerfully fanged spider—is universally feared.

   _____**Q.** Actually, the tarantula has more to fear of its enemies than it occasions in us.

   _____**R.** Its greatest foe is the female diggerwasp *Pepis*, which requires one full-grown tarantula for each egg she lays.

   _____**S.** By the time the egg's hatched larva finishes nourishing itself on the tarantula and becomes a wasp, there is nothing left of the tarantula except its indigestible skeleton.

   _____**T.** She paralyzes the target tarantula, placing it in a grave she digs until she can lay her egg and attach it to the tarantula's underbelly.

   _____**U.** The tarantula, however, is dangerous only to insects and small animals; to humans its bite is no worse than a hornet sting.

   The second sentence is   Ⓠ Ⓡ Ⓢ Ⓣ Ⓤ
   The third sentence is   Ⓠ Ⓡ Ⓢ Ⓣ Ⓤ
   The fourth sentence is   Ⓠ Ⓡ Ⓢ Ⓣ Ⓤ
   The fifth sentence is   Ⓠ Ⓡ Ⓢ Ⓣ Ⓤ
   The sixth sentence is   Ⓠ Ⓡ Ⓢ Ⓣ Ⓤ

2. Benjamin Franklin is considered the American Leonardo da Vinci, the progenitor of many diverse ideas and inventions.

_____**Q.** They do not say much about the half-glasses for reading still in use today or what he had to do with the Franklin stove.

_____**R.** Least known, perhaps, is his invention of the sport we call waterskiing.

_____**S.** He even wrote about his idea and submitted his design to a carpenter, but that was the end of it.

_____**T.** He designed a large kite capable of pulling someone across the water plus skis made from barrel staves to religious organizations for use in charitable work.

_____**U.** History books detail his political importance, his publishing successes, his part in discovering electricity, how he started the post office, and how he established the public library.

The second sentence is ⓠ ⓡ ⓢ ⓣ ⓤ
The third sentence is ⓠ ⓡ ⓢ ⓣ ⓤ
The fourth sentence is ⓠ ⓡ ⓢ ⓣ ⓤ
The fifth sentence is ⓠ ⓡ ⓢ ⓣ ⓤ
The sixth sentence is ⓠ ⓡ ⓢ ⓣ ⓤ

QUESTIONS 3–5: LOGICAL REASONING

Directions: Read each question very carefully and choose the **best** answer from the five choices given. Select your answer based **only** on the information provided.

3. All the streets and avenues in the city where Ashan lives run north-south or east-west.

To get to Ashan's house, 227 Como Street, Clark's shortest route is to walk north along Bright Street until he comes to Wells Avenue, where he makes a right (east) turn, walks two blocks, and then turns south.

James lives in the corner house at 444 Main Street, which is two blocks west of Bright Street and three blocks north of Wells Avenue.

For James to get to Ashan's house, he should walk

A. east to Como, and then make a right.

B. south to Wells, and then make a left.

C. west to Como, and then make a left.

D. east to Como, and then walk north.

E. south to Bright, and then left to Como.

4. Cory has six times as many cookies as Mike. Phil has half as many as Judy. Judy has half as many as Cory. Mike has six cookies. How many cookies does Phil have?

F. 9
G. 6
H. 12
J. 16
K. 4

In the code below each word is always represented by only one letter. The letter can be used for only one word. The letter over a word may or may not stand for that particular word. The letters in a line stand for the words in the line below.

(1) P   N   Y   Z   means

Flowers   are   usually   colorful.

(2) X   Y   N   R   means

Leaves   are   usually   green.

(3) W   R   Z   S   Y   means

Green   flowers   are   not   rare.

(4) Y   L   X   Q   N   T   means

Usually   they   are   mistaken   for   leaves.

5. What letter represents the word *usually*?

A. Y

B. Q

C. X

D. N

E. Not enough information is given in the problems code or in the sentences and letters to find a correct answer.

QUESTIONS 6–13: READING PASSAGES

Directions: Read each passage below and answer the questions that follow. Remember to **use only the information you have read in the passage** when answering the questions; you may reread the passage if necessary.

At the base of the Queensborough Bridge, the street is clear of traffic. There are two large paddy wagons, one marked Scuba Unit, several police cars,
5   an ambulance, a very large trampoline, and dozens of milling cops. Here and there on the nearby sidewalk, clusters of people gaze up at the bridge, where a searchlight moves about, searching,
10   like a spotlight that has lost the actors.

"What's going on?" asks a spectator.

"See the guy up there? He's gonna jump," says another.

Way, way up at the very top of the
15   tram tower over the bridge, a figure the size of a peanut in its shell is silhouetted against the spotlight. Not far away are cops who have slowly climbed up a long, thin ladder from the street.

20   "Wish he'd jump already," says someone.

"It's costing the city $20,000 a minute for this guy," a man says with authority.

The spectators wait for the police
25   to bring a distraught young woman to one of the trucks and hand her a microphone. Her voice choked, she will call out, "Johnny, this is Miriam. I'm sorry. Things will be different now. Just come down."

30   Or maybe it will be a middle-aged man saying, "I've got the money," or another in a starched white jacket saying, "We've made a mistake. Those were the wrong X-rays."

35   But it never happens. The cops grab the guy, they bring him down, the lights go out, traffic moves, and the spectators look disappointed.

6. Which of the following is the best title for this passage?

    F. The Suicide

    G. The Horrified Watchers

    H. A Night in the City

    J. The Wrong X-Ray

    K. The Suicide That Wasn't

7. When someone threatens to jump off a bridge in a big city,

    A. nobody is interested except the girlfriend.

    B. spectators scream and cry in anticipation.

    C. rescue units gather to stop or save the jumper.

    D. it is big news.

    E. his fiancée makes promises.

8. Which of the following best describes the spectators?

    F. Worried at first, then relieved

    G. Cynical New Yorkers looking for more excitement

    H. Trying to be helpful

    J. Frightened for the man

    K. Rallying together

9. What is the most likely reason the spectators might have expected a woman to take the microphone to call up to the man on the bridge?

    A She might frighten the man into jumping.

    B. He might have been suicidal after a fight with his girlfriend.

    C. She was a policewoman.

    D. This is how it happens in the movies.

    E. The police were too busy to round up a lot of helpful people.

Felipe Lopez, guard for his Bronx high school team, the Rice Raiders, is already doing so well that he has done a Nintendo commercial, been profiled in
5 *The New Yorker* magazine, and is being constantly scouted by college basketball teams, even with his senior year still ahead of him.

This is how Susan Orlean put it in
10 her *New Yorker* piece: "White men in suits follow Felipe Lopez everywhere he goes. . . . They rarely miss one of Felipe's games or tournaments. They have absolute recall of his best minutes of
15 play. They are authorities on his physical condition. They admire his feet, which are big and pontoon-shaped, and his wrists, which have a loose, silky motion."

Felipe, who is 6'5" tall, and still
20 growing, has remained a really likable teenage boy. He spoke no English at all when he came to New York from the Dominican Republic, but now he talks a lot, and fast. Back where he came from,
25 they look forward to his being the first Dominican in the NBA someday.

Though people who know him like him, neither are all of them eager to see him succeed, nor does everyone have his
30 best interests at heart. His father has warned him to be careful with girls who see him as a possible lucrative paternity suit. Coaches of colleges he isn't considering are interested only in their players'
35 one day beating him on the court.

And there are those who willingly trot out the odds against his dreams coming true. Of the 518,000 male basketball players in U.S. high schools
40 today, only 4 percent will end up on college teams, and of those, less than 1 percent will play for the top colleges. And only forty or fifty new players are drafted each year by the NBA.
45 That means there are a great many disappointed high school players, a disproportionate number of whom are ethnic minorities like Felipe; there are more minority than white high school
50 players who expect to play on a college team.

Felipe first played basketball in his native country, before he grew tall. He tried to dunk, but at first could not, so
55 he kept trying and trying. "Then one day I dunked. . . . Three months later, I was dunking everything every way—with two hands, backwards, backwards with two hands. I can do a three-sixty dunk,"
60 he told Orlean.

He works hard to beat those tough statistics. In basketball, he says, you are always working, "even on the things you already know."

10. "White men in suits"

   F. are reporters for newspapers.

   G. are basketball coaches.

   H. are basketball scouts.

   J. are basketball fans.

   K. hope Felipe will fail.

11. From this passage you gather that

   A. Felipe is not your average high school player.

   B. Felipe is more than just tall and hard working.

   C. some people will try to take advantage of Felipe.

   D. even with his qualifications, Felipe may not make it all the way.

   E. All of the above

12. A career as a top basketball pro

   F. becomes a reality for many high school players.

   G. is a fulfilled dream for proportionally more black kids than white ones.

   H. involves beating the odds through hard work.

   J. is possible for about 10 percent of college men each year.

   K. All of the above

13. If Felipe becomes a college player, he will

   A. quit school to play pro ball.

   B. be among the lucky 4 percent.

   C. undoubtedly make it to the pros.

   D. make everyone happy.

   E. be as outstanding a student as a player.

PART II: MATHEMATICS

13 Questions • 20 Minutes

The following information is provided for your reference. It will likely not appear in the actual test booklet. You should memorize these formulas and symbols.

FORMULAS

- Area of a circle (with radius r) = πr^2

- Circumference of a circle = $2\pi r$

- Area of a parallelogram (with base b and height h) = bh

- Area of a trapezoid (with parallel sides a and b and height h) = $\frac{1}{2}(a+b)h$

- Volume of a cone or pyramid (with base area b and height h) = $\frac{1}{3}bh$

- Volume of a cylinder (with base area b and height h) = bh

- Volume of a sphere $\left(\text{with radius } r\right)$ = $\frac{4}{3}\pi r^3$

- Sum of the measures of the angles of a triangle = $180°$

- Area of a triangle:

  $$\text{Area} = \frac{bh}{2}$$

- For a right triangle:

  $$c^2 = a^2 + b^2$$

DEFINITIONS OF SYMBOLS

= is equal to

≠ is unequal to

< is less than

> is greater than

≤ is less than or equal to

≥ is greater than or equal to

⊥ is perpendicular to

|| is parallel to

∠ angle

∟ right angle

⇉ parallel lines

NOTES

- Figures may not be drawn to scale. Do not assume any relationship in a diagram unless it is specifically stated or can be figured out from given information.

- Assume that a diagram is in one plane unless the problem specifically states that it is not.

- Reduce all fractions to lowest terms.

QUESTIONS 14–26: PROBLEM SOLVING

Directions: For each question, solve the problem and select the best answer from the choices given.

14. If $\sqrt{x+y} + A = \sqrt{x} + \sqrt{y}$, find the value of A when $x = 25$ and $y = 144$.

   F. 169
   G. 17
   H. 16
   J. 4
   K. 0

15. 15% of 300 = 4% of

   A. 800
   B. 1500
   C. 112.5
   D. 45
   E. 1125

16. Find the length of x in the figure below.

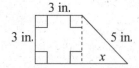

   F. 4 in.
   G. 3 in.
   H. 5 in.
   J. 7 in.
   K. None of the above

17.

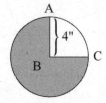

   Point B is the center of the circle. AB = 4 inches and ∠ABC is a right angle. The area of the shaded region is closest to: (use π = 3.14)

   A. 20 sq. in.
   B. 25 sq. in.
   C. 30 sq. in.
   D. 33 sq. in.
   E. 40 sq. in.

18. $70 + (-3)^2(-2)^3(-1)^4 =$

   F. $(-6)^9$
   G. 142
   H. −2
   J. −260
   K. −142

19. If $t = 9$ feet, the value of d in the formula $d = 16t^2$ is

   A. 144 sq. ft.
   B. 1296 sq. ft.
   C. 432 sq. ft.
   D. 12,960 sq. ft.
   E. 288 sq. ft.

20. Jill has an average of 87 on the first 3 exams in her physics course. What grade must she get on the fourth exam so that her average on the first 4 exams is 90?

   F. 93
   G. 95
   H. 96
   J. 97
   K. 99

21. If x is an even number, how many values of x satisfy *both* of the following conditions: $x \leq 22$ and $x > 10$?

  A. 6

  B. 7

  C. 5

  D. 8

  E. 9

22. When any number is divided by 11, the greatest possible remainder of the resulting number is

  F. 9

  G. 11

  H. 12

  J. 1

  K. 10

23. A business partnership made a profit of $16,000 one year. If one partner owned four times as many shares as the other partner, how much of the profit went to the partner with the bigger share?

  A. $12,000

  B. $4000

  C. $3200

  D. $12,800

  E. $64,000

24. In a certain boys' camp, 30% of the boys are from New York State and 20% of these are from New York City. What percent of the boys in the camp are from New York City?

  F. 60%

  G. 50%

  H. 33%

  J. 10%

  K. 6%

25.

A unit block for construction is $1 \times 2 \times 3$ inches. What is the number of whole blocks required to cover an area 1 foot long by $1\frac{1}{4}$ feet wide with *one layer* of blocks?

  A. 30 blocks

  B. 60 blocks

  C. 72 blocks

  D. 90 blocks

  E. 180 blocks

26. If the number of square inches in the area of a circle is equal to the number of inches in its circumference, the diameter of the circle is

  F. 4 inches.

  G. 2 inches.

  H. 1 inch.

  J. π inches.

  K. 2π inches.

ANSWER KEY AND EXPLANATIONS

1. UQRTS	7. C	12. H	17. E	22. K
2. UQRTS	8. G	13. B	18. H	23. D
3. A	9. B	14. J	19. B	24. K
4. F	10. H	15. R	20. K	25. A
5. D	11. E	16. F	21. A	26. F
6. K				

PART I: VERBAL
SCRAMBLED PARAGRAPHS

1. **The correct order is UQRTS.** U is the second sentence because it contradicts the fear humans have from the topic sentence. Q is third because it introduces the idea of the tarantula's enemies. R is fourth because it defines the tarantula's enemy. T is fifth because it explains what the enemy does. S is sixth because it completes the action in the fifth sentence.

2. **The correct order is UQRTS.** U is the second sentence because it gives some reasons why Franklin is considered the American da Vinci. Q is third because "they do not say" refers to the history books in the second sentence. R is fourth because "least known" follows the less-known inventions in the previous sentence. T is fifth because it describes the invention in the fourth sentence. S is sixth because it explains why this was his least-known invention.

LOGICAL REASONING

3. **The correct answer is A.** Set up a north-south, east-west grid of lines. Put Bright Street (N-S) and Wells Avenue (E-W) in the middle of your grid. Trace out Clark's walk. Now you know where Como Street is and approximately where #227 is. Paragraph three tells you where James lives—put it in. Now trace out the possible walks to find the one that gets to 227 Como Street.

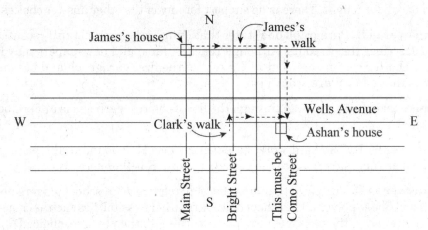

4. The correct answer is F. To find this answer:

1. Set up a table with everyone's names and cookie numbers.

2. Find the person whose cookie number is directly related to Mike's. Cory has six times as many as Mike.

3. Find the person directly related to Cory's cookie number. It is Judy who has $\frac{1}{2}$ as many as Cory.

Cory	_Mike_	_Phil_	_Judy_
1.	6 cookies		
2. $6 \times 6 = 36$	6		
3. 36		$6\frac{18}{2} = 9$	$\frac{36}{2} = 18$

5. The correct answer is D. The word _usually_ is present in sentences 1, 2, and 4. Now look for a letter present in sentences 1, 2, and 4 and not present anywhere else. The easiest way to find the correct answer is to use sentence 1 rather than sentence 4 because sentence 1 only has 4 letters to check out. P appears in no other sentence; N appears in sentences 1, 2, and 4; Y appears in 1, 2, 3, and 4; Z appears in sentences 1 and 3. The only letter that could stand for _usually_ is N.

READING PASSAGES

6. The correct answer is K. Choice F is wrong because the jumper didn't jump, and choice G is wrong because the watchers were anything but horrified. As for choice H, it was a night in the city, but not a typical one. Choice J is incorrect because it has nothing to do with the passage. Choice K is right. The passage describes a threatened suicide not completed.

7. The correct answer is C. Choice A is wrong because no girlfriend actually comes, choice B. because there was no screaming and crying, choices D and E because no mention is made of newsworthiness, and again, no fiancée comes. Choice C is right because this is detailed in the first paragraph of the passage.

8. The correct answer is G. The second choice is correct as you can tell from their comments. You might expect choice F to be true, but it is neither borne out by the piece, nor are the other choices, H, J, and K.

9. The correct answer is B. Choice B is a plausible assumption. The words the crowd expects her to say, "I'm sorry. Things will be different now," indicate the expectation that the man and the woman may have fought. There is no support for any of the other answer choices.

10. The correct answer is H. Paragraph one states that Felipe is being constantly scouted. Paragraph two describes these scouts. Although coaches, fans, and newspapers may be interested, those choices become less logical because of the first paragraph and because the description is that of a college scout's job.

11. The correct answer is E. As you read through the list of choices, each one is understood to be true as stated.

12. The correct answer is H. The hard work statement, choice H, is found in the passage. Choices F, G, and J are false according to the passage. Choice K is therefore also wrong.

13. The correct answer is B. The passage states that 4 percent of high school players now playing will become college players. The other choices are either possibilities such as choices A, C, or E, which are not in the passage, or wrong according to the passage, choice D.

Part II: Mathematics

PROBLEM SOLVING

14. The correct answer is J.

$$\sqrt{25 + 144} + A = \sqrt{25} + \sqrt{144}$$
$$\sqrt{169} + A = \sqrt{25} + \sqrt{144}$$
$$13 + A = 5 + 12 = 17$$
$$A = 4$$

15. The correct answer is E. 15% of 300 = 0.15 × 300 = 45.00

Then 45 = 4% of?

or $\dfrac{45}{0.04 *} = \dfrac{0.04x}{0.04 *}$

*Divide both sides by 0.04:

$$.04\overline{)45.00} \begin{array}{c} 1125 \\ \end{array} = x$$

$$1125 = x$$

16. The correct answer is F.

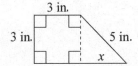

The dotted line in the square is 3". Therefore, the right triangle has these dimensions:

Use the Pythagorean theorem to find x.

$$a^2 + b^2 = c^2$$
$$3^2 + b^2 = 5^2$$
$$9 + b^2 = 25$$
$$b^2 = 16$$
$$\sqrt{b^2} = \sqrt{16}$$
$$b = 4$$

Thus, the unknown length is 4".

17. The correct answer is E. The shaded region is $\dfrac{3}{4}$ the area of the whole circle.

Thus, the shaded area $= \dfrac{3}{4} \times \pi r^2$

$$= \dfrac{3}{4} \times \pi \times 4^2 = \dfrac{3}{4} \times 16\pi = 12\pi$$

Using $\pi = 3.14$, $12\pi = (12)(3.14) = 37.68$

18. The correct answer is H.

$$70 + (-3)^2(-2)^3(-1)^4 = 70 + (9)(-8)(1) = 70 + (-72) = -2$$

19. The correct answer is B. If $d = 16t^2$ and $t = 9$, then by substitution $d = 16(9)(9) = 16(81) = 1296$ sq. ft.

20. The correct answer is K. Since Jill's average on the first 3 exams is 87, they must add up to $87 \times 3 = 261$. If her average on the first 4 exams is to be 90, they must add up to $90 \times 4 = 360$ (sum of first 3 exams) + 4th exam = (sum of first 4 exams).

$$261 + \text{4th exam} = 360$$
$$\text{4th exam} = 99$$

21. The correct answer is A. We're looking for even numbers that are greater than 10 and less than or equal to 22. These numbers are 12, 14, 16, 18, 20, and 22. That is a total of 6 numbers.

22. The correct answer is K. When dividing by 11, any whole number less than 11 may be a remainder. The greatest of these choices is 10.

23. The correct answer is D.

Let x = partner with smaller share
$4x$ = partner with larger share
therefore, $x + 4x = 16,000$

$$\frac{5x}{5} = \frac{16,000}{5} \text{ (divide both sides by 5)}$$
$$x = 3,200$$
$$4x = \$12,800$$

24. The correct answer is K. Thirty percent (0.30) of the boys are from New York State, and 20% (0.20) of them are from New York City. Therefore, 6% (0.20×0.30) of the boys in the camp are from New York City.

25. The correct answer is A. An area 1 foot long by $1\frac{1}{4}$ feet wide is 12" $\times$ 15", or 180 square inches in area. Each block is 6 square inches in area. Therefore, the number of blocks needed is $\frac{180}{6} = 30$ blocks. The height of each block is irrelevant to the solution of the problem.

26. The correct answer is F. The area of a circle is equal to πr^2. The circumference of a circle is equal to πd. If the number of inches in each are equal, then $\pi d = \pi r^2$, or the diameter equals the square of the radius. The only value for which the diameter can equal the square of the radius is a diameter of 4".

ANSWER SHEET PRACTICE TEST 8
Part I: Verbal

Scrambled Paragraphs

Paragraph 1

The second sentence is   Ⓠ Ⓡ Ⓢ Ⓣ Ⓤ

The third sentence is   Ⓠ Ⓡ Ⓢ Ⓣ Ⓤ

The fourth sentence is   Ⓠ Ⓡ Ⓢ Ⓣ Ⓤ

The fifth sentence is   Ⓠ Ⓡ Ⓢ Ⓣ Ⓤ

The sixth sentence is   Ⓠ Ⓡ Ⓢ Ⓣ Ⓤ

Paragraph 2

The second sentence is   Ⓠ Ⓡ Ⓢ Ⓣ Ⓤ

The third sentence is   Ⓠ Ⓡ Ⓢ Ⓣ Ⓤ

The fourth sentence is   Ⓠ Ⓡ Ⓢ Ⓣ Ⓤ

The fifth sentence is   Ⓠ Ⓡ Ⓢ Ⓣ Ⓤ

The sixth sentence is   Ⓠ Ⓡ Ⓢ Ⓣ Ⓤ

Logical Reasoning

3. Ⓐ Ⓑ Ⓒ Ⓓ Ⓔ
4. Ⓕ Ⓖ Ⓗ Ⓙ Ⓚ
5. Ⓐ Ⓑ Ⓒ Ⓓ Ⓔ

Reading

6. Ⓕ Ⓖ Ⓗ Ⓙ Ⓚ   9. Ⓐ Ⓑ Ⓒ Ⓓ Ⓔ   12. Ⓕ Ⓖ Ⓗ Ⓙ Ⓚ

7. Ⓐ Ⓑ Ⓒ Ⓓ Ⓔ   10. Ⓕ Ⓖ Ⓗ Ⓙ Ⓚ   13. Ⓐ Ⓑ Ⓒ Ⓓ Ⓔ

8. Ⓕ Ⓖ Ⓗ Ⓙ Ⓚ   11. Ⓐ Ⓑ Ⓒ Ⓓ Ⓔ

PART II: MATHEMATICS
PROBLEM SOLVING

14. Ⓕ Ⓖ Ⓗ Ⓙ Ⓚ   19. Ⓐ Ⓑ Ⓒ Ⓓ Ⓔ   23. Ⓐ Ⓑ Ⓒ Ⓓ Ⓔ

15. Ⓐ Ⓑ Ⓒ Ⓓ Ⓔ   20. Ⓕ Ⓖ Ⓗ Ⓙ Ⓚ   24. Ⓕ Ⓖ Ⓗ Ⓙ Ⓚ

16. Ⓕ Ⓖ Ⓗ Ⓙ Ⓚ   21. Ⓐ Ⓑ Ⓒ Ⓓ Ⓔ   25. Ⓐ Ⓑ Ⓒ Ⓓ Ⓔ

17. Ⓐ Ⓑ Ⓒ Ⓓ Ⓔ   22. Ⓕ Ⓖ Ⓗ Ⓙ Ⓚ   26. Ⓕ Ⓖ Ⓗ Ⓙ Ⓚ

18. Ⓕ Ⓖ Ⓗ Ⓙ Ⓚ

answer sheet

Practice Test 8

PART 1: VERBAL

13 Questions • 20 Minutes

QUESTIONS 1–2: SCRAMBLED PARAGRAPHS

Directions: The paragraph below consists of six sentences in scrambled order. The first, or topic, sentence is given, and you are to arrange the rest in an order that makes sense, each sentence following from the one before in that it explains the earlier one or adds to it.

Write the numbers to the left of the letters (in pencil so you can change them as often as you need). When you are satisfied, mark your choices on the answer sheet.

Because you get no partial credit for having only some of the sentences in a paragraph in order and because trying different arrangements to find which reads best requires more time than other test questions, each of the scrambled paragraphs carries twice the weight of other questions on the test.

1. For more than a century, Niagara Falls has exerted a manic challenge to men and women possessed of an excessive need for thrills.

_____**Q.** The craze to actually ride the falls in a barrel got its start when Carlisle Graham, a Philadelphia barrel maker, made it safely in 1886.

_____**R.** Since these pioneers, many daredevils have plunged over the falls in many kinds of containers, some of them making it in one piece, many not.

_____**S.** It was almost a decade later before the first American duplicated the Frenchman's feat, followed two years later by a woman who did it twice, once with wrists and ankles manacled.

_____**T.** In 1859, a French tightrope walker crossed over the crashing falls on a cable several times, one time at night by the light from a locomotive.

_____**U.** Although the light failed when he was about half way across, he managed to make it safely in the dark.

The second sentence is   Ⓠ Ⓡ Ⓢ Ⓣ Ⓤ

The third sentence is   Ⓠ Ⓡ Ⓢ Ⓣ Ⓤ

The fourth sentence is   Ⓠ Ⓡ Ⓢ Ⓣ Ⓤ

The fifth sentence is   Ⓠ Ⓡ Ⓢ Ⓣ Ⓤ

The sixth sentence is   Ⓠ Ⓡ Ⓢ Ⓣ Ⓤ

2. Before apartheid was inflicted on the black majority population of South Africa, domestic violence as we know it was kept under control by tribal custom.

_____**Q.** During the apartheid era, the clan system was broken down by white rulers who, with few exceptions, prohibited families from living together in group shelters.

_____**R.** In fact, men caught committing sexual crimes against children could be put to death by the clan or tribe—a kind of extended family united under one clan name.

_____**S.** The white rulers also treated women as minors, subordinate to men, rather than as the arbiters of tribal behavior as before.

_____**T.** As a consequence of those years, there was ever-increasing violence against women and children without an established means to prevent it.

_____**U.** Women banded together to publicly discipline men who were abusive to their wives or children, and there were strong social sanctions against men who violated sexual taboos.

The second sentence is   Ⓠ Ⓡ Ⓢ Ⓣ Ⓤ

The third sentence is   Ⓠ Ⓡ Ⓢ Ⓣ Ⓤ

The fourth sentence is   Ⓠ Ⓡ Ⓢ Ⓣ Ⓤ

The fifth sentence is   Ⓠ Ⓡ Ⓢ Ⓣ Ⓤ

The sixth sentence is   Ⓠ Ⓡ Ⓢ Ⓣ Ⓤ

QUESTIONS 3–5: LOGICAL REASONING

Directions: Read each question very carefully and choose the **best** answer from the five choices given. Select your answer based **only** on the information provided.

3. A garden has a total of sixty vegetable plants, consisting of carrots, onions, cabbages, and lettuce. All but twenty-four plants are carrots; all but half of the remainder are lettuce; only two plants are onions. How many more carrots are there than cabbages?

   A. 14

   B. 12

   C. 24

   D. 26

   E. 18

4. Five men are standing shoulder to shoulder, alternating facing north and south starting with the man on the left. If the second and third men turn right $\frac{1}{4}$ turn, then the first man turns to face the second man, and the last two in line turn left $\frac{1}{4}$ turn, how many men end up facing west?

   F. 0

   G. 1

   H. 2

   J. 3

   K. 4

The problem below uses a code where each letter always stands for one particular word present in the code. The letter always stands for that word and no other. The letters on a line stand for the words in the line just below. The letter that stands for a word may or may not be situated directly above the word it stands for.

(1) P   N   Y   Z   means

Flowers   are   usually   colorful.

(2) X   Y   N   R   means

Leaves   are   usually   green.

(3) W   R   Z   S   Y   means

Green   flowers   are   not   rare.

(4) Y   L   X   Q   N   T   means

Usually   they   are   mistaken   for   leaves.

5. Regarding the letters T, L, P, and Q, the letter or letters that can definitely be determined to stand for a particular word, given the information supplied is (are):

A. T

B. L

C. P

D. Q

E. All four choices are correct.

QUESTIONS 6–13: READING PASSAGES

Directions: Read each passage below and answer the questions that follow. Remember to **use only the information you have read in the passage** when answering the questions; you may reread the passage if necessary.

Among the notions held by the earliest thinking Greeks was the one that there was no difference between places and persons. So it seemed perfectly
5 acceptable that the personifications of Mother Earth and Father Heaven could produce offspring, the first true living creatures.

Those early creatures were, like the
10 dinosaurs we think inhabited the earth before us, monsters. At once human and superhuman, they were gigantic in size and possessed inhuman strength. Some had a hundred hands and fifty heads
15 each; others had only one enormous eye in the middle of the forehead. A third tribe, just as strong and fearsome, was not so destructive, and was even capable of goodness.

20   One of the members of this third tribe, called Titans, gave birth to the first god, Zeus. He, like all the gods of mythology, was modeled after man, but had superhuman powers. Zeus went
25 to war against the monsters and, with the help of one friendly Titan, won out, setting the stage for the creation of man. How this was accomplished is the basis of conflicting stories, but all agree that
30 for a long time Man was only man. There were no women.

Woman, in the person of Pandora, was created by Zeus in a fit of anger at men. Woman was to be their punishment.

35 She was made wondrously beautiful and femininely curious. The gods gave Pandora a box, into which they each put something, and instructed her never to open it. Too curious not to, she lifted the
40 lid, thereby releasing assorted plagues and human miseries, along with one useful gift for mankind, Hope, with which to deal with life's misfortunes. And ever since, women have brought both joy and
45 trouble to men.

6. This passage is mainly about

   F. how man, and then woman, came to be, according to ancient Greeks.

   G. how monsters once ruled earth.

   H. how evolution got started, according to Greek myth.

   J. male supremacy in early religions.

   K. how Greek gods once ruled the earth.

7. Pandora's box

   A. made the gods angry.

   B. contained plagues and miseries she was instructed to unleash.

   C. contained good gifts as well as bad, which she was supposed to sort through.

   D. probably was supposed to tempt her to open it.

   E. was Zeus' idea of a reward for men's exemplary behavior.

8. How were the Titans different from the other monster tribes?

   F. They were the earliest human beings.

   G. They were the strongest and most destructive.

   H. They were the children of the gods.

   J. They were the least destructive and most decent.

   K. They were created by Zeus.

9. The earliest thinking Greeks believed

   A. there was only one true god.

   B. places, like persons, could conceive living offspring.

   C. man needed woman.

   D. Zeus was the first man.

   E. the gods were all good and merciful.

I was once a ghostwriter. If you are a professional writer, being a ghostwriter seems more ghost than writer. What, people would ask, those who
5 had penetrated my invisibility, does a ghostwriter actually do?

Well, I would reveal, he (or she) is hired to write for somebody who knows a lot about something, but can't write
10 so anybody would want to read it. The potential author is so knowledgeable that he can get a publisher to give him an advance (money up front) for writing a book or article that will be interesting to
15 read. But when he sits down and writes some of it, the publisher says, oh no, get yourself a writer for this, and maybe gives my name. So I get the job of writing this guy's autobiography, or all he knows
20 about tuning an automobile, or how to get a girlfriend, or cooking ethnic dishes, or rehabilitating prisoners, or whatever.

Sometimes he (who is sometimes a she) gives me what he wrote and I change
25 it all around: the order, the style, the words, the length, everything except the facts or the meaning. Sometimes he just talks, and answers my questions, into a tape recorder. And too many just say:
30 "Here's the research I used. Write it."

But here is where the problem comes in. When you work your head off and get it all written up in real writing, the expert gets annoyed with it. He claims
35 you left out too much. She claims you took out her best writing: poetry to her, junk to you.

What it is, see, is they are all in love
with their own writing, no matter how bad
40 it is. Everyone, it seems, thinks himself
a writer. It's funny because not everyone
thinks she can paint a landscape or
compose a sonata or hurdle a high jump.
    What they don't know, and I hope you
45 do, is that you have to have two things
to be a writer. One is you have to have
talent—and that's probably luck, and
the other is you have to learn what good
writing does and doesn't do. You do that
50 by reading a lot, reading critically, and
by studying writing with writers. Then
you just write and write and write until
you no longer sweat it, and you enjoy cor-
recting and improving your own words.
55   I never used to let them use my
name, those clients who put back their
own junk. That's the ghost part.

10. Which of the following best tells what this
passage is about?

F. The function of a ghostwriter

G. The difficulties of being a
ghostwriter

H. How a ghostwriter learns to write

J. What ghostwriters write about

K. Ghostwriters do professional
writing

11. Which of the following is the ghost writer's
biggest complaint?

A. Interpreting information is very
difficult.

B. Publishers don't give you any credit.

C. Everyone thinks he can write.

D. Ghostwriters don't get paid enough.

E. Clients think too little about the
efforts of a ghostwriter.

12. Which of the following is stated by the
passage?

F. Anyone can be a professional writer
if he believes he can.

G. Publishers are foolish.

H. Some clients never pay.

J. Very few authors use ghostwriters.

K. Reading and writing a lot improves
your writing skills.

13. A ghostwriter

A. is hired by the publisher.

B. usually works by taking notes from
the client.

C. may be suggested to the author by
the publisher.

D. is an excellent professional writer.

E. never has his or her name used.

PART II: MATHEMATICS

13 Questions • 20 Minutes

The following information is provided for your reference. It will likely not appear in the actual test booklet. You should memorize these formulas and symbols.

FORMULAS

- Area of a circle (with radius r) = πr^2

- Circumference of a circle = $2\pi r$

- Area of a parallelogram (with base b and height h) = bh

- Area of a trapezoid (with parallel sides a and b and height h) = $\frac{1}{2}(a+b)h$

- Volume of a cone or pyramid (with base area b and height h) = $\frac{1}{3}bh$

- Volume of a cylinder (with base area b and height h) = bh

- Volume of a sphere (with radius r) = $\frac{4}{3}\pi r^3$

- Sum of the measures of the angles of a triangle = 180°

- Area of a triangle:

$$\text{Area} = \frac{bh}{2}$$

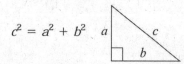

- For a right triangle:

$$c^2 = a^2 + b^2$$

DEFINITIONS OF SYMBOLS

=   is equal to

≠   is unequal to

<   is less than

>   is greater than

≤   is less than or equal to

≥   is greater than or equal to

⊥   is perpendicular to

‖   is parallel to

∠   angle

∟   right angle

⇉   parallel lines

NOTES

- Figures may not be drawn to scale. Do not assume any relationship in a diagram unless it is specifically stated or can be figured out from given information.

- Assume that a diagram is in one plane unless the problem specifically states that it is not.

- Reduce all fractions to lowest terms.

QUESTIONS 14–26: PROBLEM SOLVING

Directions: For each question, solve the problem and select the best answer from the choices given.

14. +1, 0, –1, +1, 0, –1, +1, 0, –1, . . . and so on, where the last number is +1, has a sum of

    F. +1

    G. –1

    H. +2

    J. 0

    K. –2

15. An arched window is in the shape of a rectangle with a semicircle on top. If the base of the rectangle is 14 inches and the height of the rectangle is 20 inches, find the perimeter of the whole window (use $\pi = \frac{22}{7}$).

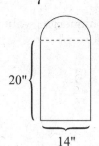

20"

14"

    A. 76 in.

    B. 280 in.

    C. 68 in.

    D. 56 in.

    E. 77 in.

16. At 12:30 p.m., what is the smaller angle between the minute hand and the hour hand?

    F. 180°

    G. 175°

    H. 165°

    J. 150°

    K. 160°

17. If Sue is x years old now and her sister is 3 years younger, then 5 years from now her sister will be what age?

    A. $x - 3$

    B. $x + 5$

    C. $x + 2$

    D. $x + 8$

    E. x

18. Mr. Diaz gets $12 an hour for doing 8 hours work, and $1\frac{1}{2}$ times that for over-time. How much does he earn if he works 12 hours?

    F. $102

    G. $108

    H. $138

    J. $144

    K. $168

19. How much greater is the volume of a cube whose edge is 5 inches than the volume of a cube whose edge is 4 inches?

    A. 125 cu. in.

    B. 61 cu. in.

    C. 64 cu. in.

    D. 9 cu. in.

    E. 1 cu. in.

20. What is the area of the shaded triangle in this square?

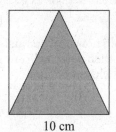

10 cm

F. 10 sq. cm.

G. 20 sq. cm.

H. 100 sq. cm.

J. 50 sq. cm.

K. None of the above

21. A jar contains 5 white marbles, 6 black marbles, and 4 green marbles. If Ann removes 3 white marbles, 2 black marbles, and 1 green marble, what is the probability that the next marble removed at random is black?

A. $\frac{4}{5}$

B. $\frac{1}{3}$

C. $\frac{4}{9}$

D. $\frac{6}{15}$

E. $\frac{4}{15}$

22. $\frac{5}{16} \times \frac{1}{2} + \frac{3}{8} =$

F. $\frac{17}{32}$

G. $\frac{35}{128}$

H. $\frac{8}{32}$

J. 1

K. $\frac{15}{256}$

23. A man standing at point A walks 1 mile south, 3 miles east, 5 miles north, and 7 miles west to reach point B. The length of line segment $\overline{AB}$ is

A. 4 miles

B. $\sqrt{8}$ miles

C. 2 miles

D. $\sqrt{32}$ miles

E. $\sqrt{12}$ miles

24. The least common multiple of 20, 24, and 32 is

F. 240

G. 480

H. 960

J. 1920

K. 15,360

25. If $9x + 5 = 23$, the numerical value of $18x + 5$ is

A. 46

B. 41

C. 38

D. 36

E. 32

26. When fractions $\frac{2}{3}, \frac{5}{7}, \frac{8}{11},$ and $\frac{9}{13}$ are arranged in ascending order of size, the result is

F. $\frac{8}{11}, \frac{5}{7}, \frac{9}{13}, \frac{2}{3}$

G. $\frac{5}{7}, \frac{8}{11}, \frac{2}{3}, \frac{9}{13}$

H. $\frac{2}{3}, \frac{8}{11}, \frac{5}{7}, \frac{9}{13}$

J. $\frac{2}{3}, \frac{9}{13}, \frac{5}{7}, \frac{8}{11}$

K. $\frac{9}{13}, \frac{2}{3}, \frac{8}{11}, \frac{5}{7}$

ANSWER KEY AND EXPLANATIONS

1. TUSQR	7. D	12. K	17. C	22. F
2. URQST	8. J	13. C	18. K	23. D
3. D	9. B	14. F	19. B	24. G
4. H	10. F	15. A	20. J	25. B
5. C	11. C	16. H	21. C	26. J
6. F				

PART I: VERBAL
SCRAMBLED PARAGRAPHS

1. **The correct order is TUSQR.** T is the second sentence because it describes the first "manic challenge" in the topic sentence. U is third because it continues the action in the second sentence. S is fourth because it refers to the Frenchman's feat. Q is fifth because the other remaining sentence R has to be the concluding sentence. R is sixth because it sums up everything.

2. **The correct order is URQST.** U is the second sentence because it explains how tribal custom worked. R is third because it continues the description in the second sentence. Q is fourth because it introduces what apartheid did, as mentioned in the topic sentence. S is fifth because "also" in "white rulers also" shows that it finishes the thought in the fourth sentence. T is sixth because it concludes the statement in the topic sentence.

LOGICAL REASONING

3. **The correct answer is D.** Make a table of all given information, like the one shown below. Now find the cabbages. 36 + 12 + 2 = all others = 50; therefore, cabbages = 10. Last step: 36 − 10 = 26.

Vegetables	Carrots	Lettuce	Onions	Cabbages
Total: 60	60 − 24 = 36	$\frac{1}{2}$ of 24 = 12	2	60 − 50 = 10

4. **The correct answer is H.** Set up a diagram of the situation presented, like the one below. Put in the moves of each man. Count the west-facing arrows. Remember that west and left are the same position; north is always up unless otherwise stated.

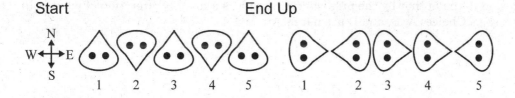

5. **The correct answer is C.** The first thing to do is to locate the sentences where P, L, Q, and T appear. What is the same for all four letters is that they all show up only once. Further study reveals that L, Q, and T are all in sentence 4. Therefore, which letter stands for which of the three words in sentence 4 that only appear in sentence 4 is not possible. On the other hand, P is the only letter in sentence 1 that appears only once and therefore must stand for the word in sentence 1 that appears only once. That word is *colorful*; P is the correct answer.

READING PASSAGES

6. **The correct answer is F.** Choice G is wrong because monsters did not actually rule earth, and choice H is wrong because the early Greeks' explanation is not evolution, neither is it implied here. Choice J is wrong because early religions are not discussed, neither is choice K. Choice F is correct because this passage does tell how ancient Greeks explained the origin of man and woman.

7. **The correct answer is D.** Choice A is wrong; an angry god made the box, not vice versa, and choice B is wrong because the passage said she was told not to open the box. Choice C is not even a consideration, and choice E is the reverse of what is described. So we can infer that choice D is right from the fact that Pandora was created curious and to punish men.

8. **The correct answer is J.** Choice F is wrong because the Titans came before gods or humans. Choice G is the opposite of what is said here. Choice H is also wrong; they were the children of Heaven and Earth, parents of the gods. And they were not created by Zeus, but he by them. The correct answer is choice J, which is stated in the last sentence of paragraph two.

9. **The correct answer is B.** Choices A, C, and D are all the opposite of what the passage states. This is true of choice E as well; merciful gods do not seek revenge upon all men. So choice B is correct; they thought Heaven and Earth could produce offspring.

10. **The correct answer is F.** Although choices G, H, and J are all part of the passage, they are more or less equally touched upon. Look at paragraph one; it ends with "(what) does a ghostwriter actually do?"

11. **The correct answer is C.** The complaint is that people who hire ghostwriters think too highly of their writing and want to retain the writing that the ghostwriter knows is garbage. All other choices are not part of the passage.

12. **The correct answer is K.** Paragraph six states that you learn to write well by reading and writing a lot. Choices G, H, and J are not supported by the passage, and choice F is a misinterpretation of what is said.

13. **The correct answer is C.** It is stated in paragraph two that a ghostwriter may be suggested to the author by the publisher. Choice E is a misinterpretation of what is in the passage. Choices A, B, and D are not mentioned.

Part II: Mathematics

PROBLEM SOLVING

14. The correct answer is F. $+1, 0, -1, \quad +1, 0, -1, \quad +1, 0, -1, \quad \ldots +1 = +1$

$\underbrace{}_{0} \quad \underbrace{}_{0} \quad \underbrace{}_{0}$

(every three numbers add up to 0 except the last + 1)

15. The correct answer is A.

perimeter = 20 + 14 + 20 + semicircle

$= 54 + \dfrac{1}{2}$ circumference

$= 54 + \dfrac{1}{2} \times \pi \times$ diameter

$= 54 + \dfrac{1}{\cancel{2}} \times \dfrac{\overset{11}{\cancel{22}}}{7} \times \overset{2}{\cancel{14}}$

$= 54 + 22 = 76$

16. The correct answer is H.

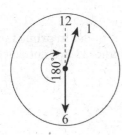

A clock is a circle containing 360°. From the 12 to the 6 there are 180°. From the 12 to the 1 there are 30°. At 12:30, the hour hand is halfway between the 12 and the 1. One half of 30° is 15°. Therefore, the smaller angle between the minute hand and the hour hand is 180° − 15° = 165°.

17. The correct answer is C.

Let $x =$ Sue
$x - 3 =$ her sister $\Big\}$ present ages

Therefore, $x + 5 =$ Sue's age 5 years from now, and $(x - 3) + 5 =$ her sister's age 5 years from now. $(x - 3) + 5 = x + 2$

18. The correct answer is K. $12 an hour for 8 hours = $96

$12 × 1.5 = $18 an hour for 4 hours = $72

$96 + 72 = $168

19. The correct answer is B. Volume of a cube $= e^3 = e \times e \times e$

Cube with edge 5 in. $= 5 \times 5 \times 5 = 125$ cu. in.

Cube with edge 4 in. $= 4 \times 4 \times 4 = 64$ cu. in.

Subtract: 125 − 64 = 61 cu. in.

20. The correct answer is J. Area of a triange $= \dfrac{bh}{2}$

Since the triangle is inside the square, the height is 10 cm.

Area $= \dfrac{1}{2} \times 10 \times 10 = 50$ sq cm

21. The correct answer is C. After Ann removes the 3 white, 2 black, and 1 green marbles, the jar contains 2 white + 4 black + 3 green marbles = a total of 9 marbles.

The probability that a marble chosen at random from these 9 marbles is black is

$$\frac{4 \text{ black}}{9 \text{ total}} = \frac{4}{9}$$

22. The correct answer is F.

$$\frac{5}{16} \times \frac{1}{2} = \frac{5}{32}$$

$$\frac{5}{32} + \frac{3}{8} = \frac{5}{32} + \frac{12}{32} = \frac{17}{32}$$

23. The correct answer is D.

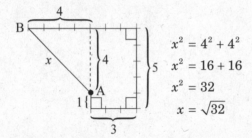

$$x^2 = 4^2 + 4^2$$
$$x^2 = 16 + 16$$
$$x^2 = 32$$
$$x = \sqrt{32}$$

24. The correct answer is G. The LCM is found by rewriting each number in prime factorization and finding the product of each unique prime factor. 22 and 23 are not selected because each is a factor of 2^5.

$$20 = 2^2 \cdot 5$$
$$24 = 2^3 \cdot 3$$
$$32 = 2^5$$
$$\text{LCM} = 5 \cdot 3 \cdot 2^5 = 480$$

Trial and error can also give you this answer. None of the other choices can be divided by all three numbers without a remainder.

25. The correct answer is B. If $9x + 5 = 23$, then $9x = 18$, and $x = 2$. Therefore, $18x + 5$ equals $18(2) + 5 = 41$.

26. The correct answer is J. Fractions are most easily compared by comparing cross-products. Start by comparing $\frac{2}{3}$ with $\frac{5}{7}$. The product of 3 and 5 is 15. The product of 7 and 2 is 14. Therefore, $\frac{5}{7}$ is larger than $\frac{2}{3}$. Continue this process with the other fractions to be compared.

$\frac{5}{7}$ ⊠ $\frac{8}{11}$, note $\frac{8}{11} > \frac{5}{7}$ and also $\frac{8}{11} > \frac{2}{3}$

$\frac{8}{11}$ ⊠ $\frac{9}{13}$, note $\frac{8}{11} > \frac{9}{13}$

$\frac{2}{3}$ ⊠ $\frac{9}{13}$, note $\frac{9}{13} > \frac{2}{3}$ and also $\frac{9}{13} < \frac{5}{7}$

Therefore, $\frac{2}{3} < \frac{9}{13} < \frac{5}{7} < \frac{8}{11}$.

ANSWER SHEET PRACTICE TEST 9
Part I: Verbal

Scrambled Paragraphs

Paragraph 1

The second sentence is   Ⓠ Ⓡ Ⓢ Ⓣ Ⓤ

The third sentence is   Ⓠ Ⓡ Ⓢ Ⓣ Ⓤ

The fourth sentence is   Ⓠ Ⓡ Ⓢ Ⓣ Ⓤ

The fifth sentence is   Ⓠ Ⓡ Ⓢ Ⓣ Ⓤ

The sixth sentence is   Ⓠ Ⓡ Ⓢ Ⓣ Ⓤ

Paragraph 2

The second sentence is   Ⓠ Ⓡ Ⓢ Ⓣ Ⓤ

The third sentence is   Ⓠ Ⓡ Ⓢ Ⓣ Ⓤ

The fourth sentence is   Ⓠ Ⓡ Ⓢ Ⓣ Ⓤ

The fifth sentence is   Ⓠ Ⓡ Ⓢ Ⓣ Ⓤ

The sixth sentence is   Ⓠ Ⓡ Ⓢ Ⓣ Ⓤ

Logical Reasoning

3. Ⓐ Ⓑ Ⓒ Ⓓ Ⓔ
4. Ⓕ Ⓖ Ⓗ Ⓙ Ⓚ
5. Ⓐ Ⓑ Ⓒ Ⓓ Ⓔ

Reading

6. Ⓕ Ⓖ Ⓗ Ⓙ Ⓚ   9. Ⓐ Ⓑ Ⓒ Ⓓ Ⓔ   12. Ⓕ Ⓖ Ⓗ Ⓙ Ⓚ

7. Ⓐ Ⓑ Ⓒ Ⓓ Ⓔ   10. Ⓕ Ⓖ Ⓗ Ⓙ Ⓚ   13. Ⓐ Ⓑ Ⓒ Ⓓ Ⓔ

8. Ⓕ Ⓖ Ⓗ Ⓙ Ⓚ   11. Ⓐ Ⓑ Ⓒ Ⓓ Ⓔ

PART II: MATHEMATICS
PROBLEM SOLVING

14. Ⓕ Ⓖ Ⓗ Ⓙ Ⓚ   19. Ⓐ Ⓑ Ⓒ Ⓓ Ⓔ   23. Ⓐ Ⓑ Ⓒ Ⓓ Ⓔ

15. Ⓐ Ⓑ Ⓒ Ⓓ Ⓔ   20. Ⓕ Ⓖ Ⓗ Ⓙ Ⓚ   24. Ⓕ Ⓖ Ⓗ Ⓙ Ⓚ

16. Ⓕ Ⓖ Ⓗ Ⓙ Ⓚ   21. Ⓐ Ⓑ Ⓒ Ⓓ Ⓔ   25. Ⓐ Ⓑ Ⓒ Ⓓ Ⓔ

17. Ⓐ Ⓑ Ⓒ Ⓓ Ⓔ   22. Ⓕ Ⓖ Ⓗ Ⓙ Ⓚ   26. Ⓕ Ⓖ Ⓗ Ⓙ Ⓚ

18. Ⓕ Ⓖ Ⓗ Ⓙ Ⓚ

answer sheet

Practice Test 9

PART 1: VERBAL

13 Questions • 20 Minutes

QUESTIONS 1–2: SCRAMBLED PARAGRAPHS

Directions: The paragraph below consists of six sentences in scrambled order. The first, or topic, sentence is given, and you are to arrange the rest in an order that makes sense, each sentence following from the one before in that it explains the earlier one or adds to it.

Write the numbers to the left of the letters (in pencil so you can change them as often as you need). When you are satisfied, mark your choices on the answer sheet.

Because you get no partial credit for having only some of the sentences in a paragraph in order and because trying different arrangements to find which reads best requires more time than other test questions, each of the scrambled paragraphs carries twice the weight of other questions on the test.

1. In recent years, the United States has seemed plagued by natural disasters, with a resultant loss of life and property.

_____**Q.** Yet these disasters are referred to by ecologists as natural disturbances—events that from the beginning of life on our planet have created the environment that supports human and animal life and the plants that feed both.

_____**R.** Hurricanes, which have battered and flooded shore towns and barrier islands, have been equally deadly and expensive.

_____**S.** Unfortunately, people continually challenge and upset nature by continuing to build homes close to beaches and woodlands.

_____**T.** Large, slow-burning forest fires, the flooding and rebuilding of barrier islands, and the filling and draining of estuaries would be not only harmless, but also beneficial.

_____**U.** Huge forest fires—some of them encroaching upon settled areas and others destroying millions of acres of parkland, including the one in Yellowstone National Park—have been battled long and hard with varying degrees of success.

The second sentence is ⓠ ⓡ ⓢ ⓣ ⓤ
The third sentence is ⓠ ⓡ ⓢ ⓣ ⓤ
The fourth sentence is ⓠ ⓡ ⓢ ⓣ ⓤ
The fifth sentence is ⓠ ⓡ ⓢ ⓣ ⓤ
The sixth sentence is ⓠ ⓡ ⓢ ⓣ ⓤ

2. There are many methods of producing a well-written paper, but none of those methods consists of merely listing your facts and handing in your paper.

_____**Q.** The best writing results from patient rewriting, even if the revising is done in your head before starting to write.

_____**R.** Many throw out the first draft, secure in the knowledge that the important parts will stick with them and what doesn't is extraneous.

_____**S.** Acquaintance with some of the techniques used by professional writers can help you improve your own writing.

_____**T.** Some writers approach each piece by putting down everything that comes into their heads regarding the subject, not bothering to organize, capitalize, or punctuate.

_____**U.** Other writers may start by writing their lead sentence or paragraph over and over until it seems right to them and sets the style for the whole.

The second sentence is   Ⓠ Ⓡ Ⓢ Ⓣ Ⓤ
The third sentence is   Ⓠ Ⓡ Ⓢ Ⓣ Ⓤ
The fourth sentence is   Ⓠ Ⓡ Ⓢ Ⓣ Ⓤ
The fifth sentence is   Ⓠ Ⓡ Ⓢ Ⓣ Ⓤ
The sixth sentence is   Ⓠ Ⓡ Ⓢ Ⓣ Ⓤ

QUESTIONS 3–5: LOGICAL REASONING

Directions: Read each question very carefully and choose the **best** answer from the five choices given. Select your answer based **only** on the information provided.

3. Mr. and Mrs. Smith got married and had four children. Their son Pablo was born when their son Marc was eleven months old. Pablo is younger than their daughter Rebecca. Their son Roberto was their firstborn. Ruben is Mrs. Smith's son from a previous marriage. The children were born in 1975, 1979, 1982, 1984, and 1985. Who was born in 1984?

A. Rebecca

B. Pablo

C. Marc

D. Ruben

E. Roberto

4. Ann, Jan, and Fran have fifteen children altogether. Eight are boys. Ann has three boys and Jan has an equal number of girls. Jan has one more child than Fran, who has four. How many girls does Ann have?

F. 0

G. 1

H. 2

J. 3

K. 4

Question 5 below involves a code where, (1) each letter of the alphabet used represents a specific word, no matter now often the word is used; (2) a word ending with the vowel a, e, i, o, or u *cannot* be represented by a letter that is one of the above vowels; and (3) the letter representing a word may or may not be directly above the word.

(1) s	i	u	m	o	e	means
Far	apart	are	tooth	and	toe.	

(2) d	y	p	q	e		means
Distant	the	eye	and	thigh.		

(3) i	d	f	q	e		means
Close	the	teeth	and	eyes.		

(4) a	x	s	i	e		means
Closest	are	teeth	and	tongue.		

5. Which letter represents the word *closest*?

A. a

B. s

C. x

D. i

E. Cannot be determined from the information given.

QUESTIONS 6–13: READING PASSAGES

Directions: Read each passage below and answer the questions that follow. Remember to **use only the information you have read in the passage** when answering the questions; you may reread the passage if necessary.

Early in the eighteenth century, the most famous satirist of the day, Jonathan Swift, used his writing gift as a propaganda tool in the fight against injustice.
5 One of the injustices he sought to correct was the oppression of poor Irish by the English, a condition perceived to be still in force today.

Tongue fitted firmly in cheek, Swift
10 recommended a solution so graphically and gruesomely described as to make for very hard reading and even harder amusement.

First, Swift calculated the number of
15 Irish children whose parents were not able to afford to bring them up properly, using the process of elimination to do so. How could they be made to support themselves?

"They can very seldom pick up a
20 livelihood by stealing till they arrive at six years old . . . although I confess they learn the rudiments much earlier, during which time they can however be looked upon only as probationers . . .
25 "I shall now therefore humbly propose my own thoughts, which I hope will not be liable to the least objection. I have been assured by a very knowing American of my acquaintance in London
30 that a young healthy child well nursed is at a year old a most delicious, nourishing, and wholesome food, whether stewed, roasted, baked, or boiled; and I make no doubt that it will equally serve in a fric-
35 assee or a ragout," when sold to the rich.

Swift takes his gory proposition to ever-increasing lengths for many pages, finally concluding by declaring no motive
40 other "than the public good of my country, by advancing our trade, providing for infants, relieving the poor, and giving some pleasure to the rich. I have no children by which I can propose to get a single penny; the youngest being nine
45 years old, and my wife past childbearing."

6. Which of the following is the best title for this passage?

F. Solving the Irish Problem

G. Children Who Steal

H. The History of the Poor

J. Swift the Economist

K. The Writings of Jonathan Swift

7. Swift used satire to

A. get back at the Irish.

B. make money.

C. entertain the English.

D. make fun of children.

E. help fight injustice.

8. From this passage, which of the following can we tell of Swift?

F. He was concerned for the rich.

G. He hated children.

H. He was a revolutionary who had in mind the overthrow of the English government.

J. He was horrified by how the English treated poor Irish families.

K. He was an unsuccessful writer who hated the English.

9. Judging by this passage, satire makes its point by

A. giving lots of facts.

B. exaggerating its subject to make a case through the humor it invokes.

C. portraying an accurate picture of its subject so all can recognize it.

D. being silly.

E. writing in an old-fashioned style.

When a newborn arrives in our home, we all peer closely at it, even make faces and noises at it, in an unconscious effort to entertain the small creature. We do
5 not know at what point the infant can actually see, but we are told that for weeks, perhaps months, it cannot focus its eyes.

Once the baby's eyes start following
10 an object we move before it, we know the baby "sees." But what do we mean by the word—that this small creature looks at the looming nose of this mother as she gets close to him or at a picture book,
15 and sees respectively Mother or picture of a rabbit and could so name them if he had the words?

How about a middle-aged woman, blind since birth or infancy, whose eye-
20 sight, thanks to medical progress, has been surgically restored? She can see for the first time in forty years. How marvelous, we think. But is it?

Scientists have long known that
25 seeing requires more than unimpaired eyes. It requires a section of the brain's cortex, the visual center (which in a normal adult occupies half the brain) to function as well, in order that we can
30 make sense of what we see. The tiny brain of the newborn is "equipotential"—able to adapt to any form of perception. And the parts of the brain work like muscles, getting stronger and larger with use,
35 shriveling from inactivity.

So we can assume the woman blinded in babyhood developed tactile and auditory forms of perception, enlarging those sections of her brain, while the

40 visual cortex remained small. She constructed her whole life around feeling, hearing, and sensing the world around her. And maybe she did very well.

Doctors who have worked with such
45 blind people suddenly made sighted have found that most of them do not respond to the gift of sight with ease and joy. Their visual cortex, not so ready as a baby's, cannot make out what they are
50 seeing. Often the effort of adjusting from dependence on their other senses overwhelms them and, in some cases, has led to depression, illness, and early death.

10. Which of the following best describes the main idea of the passage?

   F. The importance of the visual cortex in seeing

   G. The amazing capacities of the human infant

   H. Sight in the young and old

   J. Hearing and feeling in blind humans

   K. Perception: its auditory and tactile elements

11. We know a baby can first see when

   A. the eyes stay open.

   B. the visual cortex dominates the auditory and tactile centers.

   C. equipotentiality is overcome by vision.

   D. the auditory and tactile centers develop.

   E. the eyes can focus enough to follow an object.

12. In a middle-aged or older adult blind since early childhood,

   F. the visual cortex has overcome the rest of the brain.

   G. the auditory and tactile centers of the cortex are the same size as the visual center.

   H. the visual center has shriveled away completely.

   J. the auditory and tactile areas are unusually well developed.

   K. it is unimportant where he (or she) sits in the movies.

13. When older people who have been blind since birth have their sight restored, the difficulty of interpreting what they see

   A. doesn't change their joy at what they see.

   B. makes them ask a lot of questions.

   C. may have serious negative mental and physical consequences.

   D. makes them deaf.

   E. may lead to faltering intelligence as well as tactile degeneration.

PART II: MATHEMATICS
13 Questions • 20 Minutes

The following information is provided for your reference. It will likely not appear in the actual test booklet. You should memorize these formulas and symbols.

FORMULAS

- Area of a circle (with radius r) = πr^2

- Circumference of a circle = $2\pi r$

- Area of a parallelogram (with base b and height h) = bh

- Area of a trapezoid (with parallel sides a and b and height h) $= \frac{1}{2}(a+b)h$

- Volume of a cone or pyramid (with base area b and height h) $= \frac{1}{3}bh$

- Volume of a cylinder (with base area b and height h) = bh

- Volume of a sphere $\left(\text{with radius } r\right) = \frac{4}{3}\pi r^3$

- Sum of the measures of the angles of a triangle = 180°

- Area of a triangle:

  Area $= \dfrac{bh}{2}$

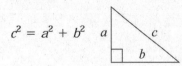

- For a right triangle:

  $c^2 = a^2 + b^2$

DEFINITIONS OF SYMBOLS

= is equal to

≠ is unequal to

< is less than

> is greater than

≤ is less than or equal to

≥ is greater than or equal to

⊥ is perpendicular to

∥ is parallel to

∠ angle

∟ right angle

⇉ parallel lines

NOTES

- Figures may not be drawn to scale. Do not assume any relationship in a diagram unless it is specifically stated or can be figured out from given information.

- Assume that a diagram is in one plane unless the problem specifically states that it is not.

- Reduce all fractions to lowest terms.

QUESTIONS 14–26: PROBLEM SOLVING

Directions: For each question, solve the problem and select the best answer from the choices given.

14. In the figure shown, the circle lies inside the square and touches each side. Each side of the square is 6 centimeters long. The area of the shaded region is closest to: (use $\pi = 3.14$)

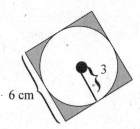

- **F.** 7 sq. cm
- **G.** 8 sq. cm
- **H.** 9 sq. cm
- **J.** 10 sq. cm
- **K.** 11 sq. cm

15. The area of a rectangle is 15 square feet, and one of the sides is 1 foot 8 inches. What is the length of the other side?

- **A.** 25 in.
- **B.** 9 ft.
- **C.** 10 ft.
- **D.** 12 ft.
- **E.** 15 ft.

16. If $x = -5$ and $y = 4$, then the value of $x^2y - y^2x$ is

- **F.** 180
- **G.** 18
- **H.** 20
- **J.** 60
- **K.** 0

17. If $9 - 3x = 3x - 9$, then $x =$

- **A.** 0
- **B.** 6
- **C.** 9
- **D.** 3
- **E.** None of the above

18. If 10 men build a 6-room house in 30 days, how many days will it take 15 men working at the same rate to build the same house?

- **F.** 180
- **G.** 25
- **H.** 45
- **J.** 20
- **K.** 15

19.

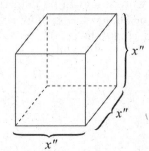

If the volume of the cube in cubic inches is equal to the total surface area of the cube in square inches, then $x =$

- **A.** 1
- **B.** 4
- **C.** 5
- **D.** 6
- **E.** 7

20. In an isosceles right triangle, the measures of the two base angles are

F. 30° and 60°

G. 45° each

H. 40° and 50°

J. 20° and 70°

K. 50° each

21.

A   B   C DE   F
←————|————|————||————→
    −5   −2   1   3 4   7

In this number line, point C is $\frac{3}{4}$ of the way from point A to point

A. F

B. B

C. C

D. D

E. E

22. In testing light bulbs, 0.15% of all bulbs in a factory were found to be defective. In an order of 36,000 bulbs, how many might be expected to be good?

F. 54

G. 5400

H. 35,946

J. 30,600

K. None of the above

23. The length of a rectangle is 8 feet and its width is 4 feet. The area of a square that has the same perimeter as that of the rectangle is

A. 36 sq. ft.

B. 24 sq. ft.

C. 32 sq. ft.

D. 48 sq. ft.

E. 64 sq. ft.

24. In two days, a point on the earth's surface rotates through an angle of approximately

F. 90°

G. 180°

H. 360°

J. 480°

K. 720°

25. Which of the following groups is arranged in order from smallest to largest?

A. $\frac{3}{7}, \frac{11}{23}, \frac{15}{32}, \frac{1}{2}, \frac{9}{16}$

B. $\frac{3}{7}, \frac{15}{32}, \frac{11}{23}, \frac{1}{2}, \frac{9}{16}$

C. $\frac{11}{23}, \frac{3}{7}, \frac{15}{32}, \frac{1}{2}, \frac{9}{16}$

D. $\frac{15}{32}, \frac{1}{2}, \frac{3}{7}, \frac{11}{23}, \frac{9}{16}$

E. $\frac{1}{2}, \frac{5}{32}, \frac{3}{7}, \frac{11}{23}, \frac{9}{16}$

26. This square has a side of 1". The diagonal distance from one corner to another is

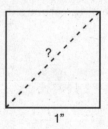

1"

F. 1 inch.

G. $\sqrt{2}$ inches.

H. $\sqrt{3}$ inches.

J. 2 inches.

K. 3 inches.

ANSWER KEY AND EXPLANATIONS

1. URQTS	7. E	12. J	17. D	22. H
2. QSTRU	8. J	13. C	18. J	23. A
3. C	9. B	14. G	19. D	24. K
4. J	10. F	15. B	20. G	25. B
5. C	11. E	16. F	21. D	26. G
6. F				

PART I: VERBAL
SCRAMBLED PARAGRAPHS

1. **The correct order is URQTS.** U is the second sentence because it describes one kind of natural disaster. R could go there too, but it says "equally deadly and expensive," so U has to precede it. R is therefore third, following the thought. Q is fourth because "yet these disasters," referring to those detailed above, presents another point of view. T is fifth because it continues the thought of the fourth sentence. S is sixth because it says why the natural benefits of fires and floods cannot be.

2. **The correct order is QSTRU.** Q is the second sentence because it says why the method in the topic sentence doesn't work. S is third because it introduces the usefulness of professional writing techniques. T is fourth because it gives one technique of writers. R is fifth because it continues about the technique in the fourth sentence. U is sixth because it starts off with "other writers" and mentions another technique.

LOGICAL REASONING

3. **The correct answer is C.** Write down the names of the children, and note that Pablo was born when Marc was 11 months old; so put them next to each other. Rebecca is older than Pablo and therefore Marc as well—put her next to Marc. Roberto was firstborn, so he is the oldest. Finally, Ruben is older than Roberto because he is from a previous marriage.

Youngest	Pablo	Marc	Rebecca	Roberto	Ruben	Oldest
	1985	1984	1982	1979	1975	

Put in the years they were born, with 1985 representing the youngest child. The easier way to solve this problem is to see that since Pablo and Marc are eleven months apart, they had to be born in the same year or in two adjoining years. Only 1985 and 1984 fit this requirement. Therefore, Marc, who is older than Pablo, was born in 1984.

4. **The correct answer is J.** Write down the names of the three mothers (see below). Next, you are told that eight children are boys, and since sentence one lets you know that there were fifteen children, seven are girls. The next sentence tells you that Ann has three boys and Jan has three girls, so put this information down under their names. Next, you are told that Jan has five children—enter this into your table. Now you can see that Jan must have two boys, and, since the total number of boys is eight, Fran must have three boys and one girl. Finally, Ann has the rest of the girls: 7 − 4 = 3.

	Ann	Jan	Fran
Boys—8	3	2	3
Girls—7	3	3	1
Total—15	6	5	4

5. **The correct answer is C.** The word *closest* only appears in sentence 4 as does the word *tongue*. By eliminating the letters *s*, *i*, and *c* because these letters appear in other sentences, we are left with the letters *a* and *x* and the words *tongue* and *closest*. Since *tongue* ends in *e*, the letter *a* cannot stand for tongue according to rule 3 of the code for this problem. So, the letter *a* must stand for *closest*, which leaves the letter *x* to stand for *tongue*.

READING PASSAGES

6. **The correct answer is F.** Choice F is right: this was Swift's tongue-in-cheek suggestion for dealing with starving Irish children. Choice G was mentioned, but is not the main idea, and choice H is wrong because the passage has nothing to do with the history of poverty. Choices J and K are wrong because Swift did not even pretend to be an economist here, and this is not about all of Swift's writing.

7. **The correct answer is E.** Choice A is wrong because he wanted to help the Irish. While choice B may be right, it is not stated in the passage. As for choice C, while it did entertain, it is not the purpose implied here. Choice D is wrong because he wanted to help poor children, leaving choice E, which is the purpose stated in the first paragraph of the passage.

8. **The correct answer is J.** Choice A is wrong; Swift made fun of the rich. Choice G is wrong because Swift was not making fun of children, only of their heartless tormentors. Nowhere is choice H stated or implied, and choice K is wrong because the passage says he was the most famous satirist of his day. We can see through the piece and tell that choice J is the right answer here.

9. **The correct answer is B.** Choice A is wrong because there are no facts here as such, and choice C is wrong because the whole piece is a deliberate exaggeration, without being silly, choice D. Choice E is wrong because the writing was very modern at the time. So, choice B is the right answer.

10. **The correct answer is F.** This is a tough question and determining the main idea really involves elimination of answers that aren't entirely correct. Choices J and K can be eliminated quickly; they say almost the same thing about one aspect of the passage. Choice H is too general and so is choice G. From beginning to end the passage deals with the visual cortex of the brain, so choice F is the best answer.

11. **The correct answer is E.** The passage states that the baby sees when the infant follows an object. This is not an easy question, to be sure, but the other answers can be eliminated as not in the passage, misinterpretations, or inferences that are too remote to hold up.

12. **The correct answer is J.** The next-to-last paragraph directly states that hearing and feeling centers are well developed in blind adults. The other answers are wrong or irrelevant except for choice H, which may be true, yet a "small" visual cortex is not an absent one.

13. **The correct answer is C.** The last paragraph emphatically states that restoration of sight can have the negative effects stated in choice C. Choice B might be true, but it is not stated in the passage. Choices A, D, and E have no credence.

Part II: Mathematics

PROBLEM SOLVING

14. The correct answer is G.

$$\text{Area of square} = 6^2 = 36$$
$$\text{Area of circle} = \pi \times 3^2$$
$$= \pi \times 9$$
$$= (3.14)(9) = 28.26$$

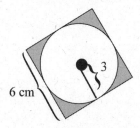

6 cm

$$\text{Area of shaded region} = \text{Area of square} - \text{Area of circle}$$
$$= 36 - 28.26 = 7.74$$

15. The correct answer is B. Area = $l \times w$

If the area is 15 square feet, we must divide by 1 ft. 8. in to find the missing side.

1 ft. 8 in. = $1\frac{2}{3}$ ft: = $\frac{5}{3}$ ft.

Therefore, $15 \div \frac{5}{3} = 15 \times \frac{3}{5} = 9$ ft.

16. The correct answer is F.

$$x^2y - y^2x = (-5)^2(4) - (4)^2(-5)$$
$$= (25)(4) - (16)(-5)$$
$$= 100 - (-80)$$
$$= 100 + 80 = 180$$

17. The correct answer is D.

$$9 - 3x = 3x - 9$$
$$9 = 6x - 9$$
$$18 = 6x$$
$$3 = x$$

18. The correct answer is J. $\frac{15\,\text{men}}{10\,\text{men}} = \frac{3}{2}$ as many men would need $\frac{2}{3}$ as many days, $\frac{2}{3}$

of 30 days = 20; or (10 men)(30 days) = (15 men)(x days), $300 = 15x$, $x = 20$

19. The correct answer is D.

$$\text{volume} = x^2$$
$$\text{total surface} = 6x^2 \,(6\,\text{square faces})$$
$$x^2 = 6x^2$$
$$x = 6$$

20. The correct answer is G. An isosceles right triangle consists of a *right* angle and two 45° angles.

21. The correct answer is D.

$$
\begin{array}{cccccc}
A & B & C & DE & F \\
\end{array}
$$

A	B	C	DE	F

$$-5 \quad -2 \quad 1 \quad 3\,4 \quad 7$$

Distance from Point A to Point C is $1 - (-5) = 6$.

Therefore, $6 = \dfrac{3}{4}x$.

Multiply both sides by $\dfrac{4}{3}$

$$\left(\frac{4}{3}\right)\frac{6}{1} = \frac{3}{4}\left(\frac{4}{3}\right)$$

$$8 = x$$

If the total distance must be 8, the other point is D.

22. The correct answer is H. 0.15% as a decimal = 0.0015

Therefore, $36{,}000 \times 0.0015 = 54$ (number of defective bulbs).

Subtract to find the number of good bulbs: $36{,}000 - 54 = 35{,}946$

23. The correct answer is A. The perimeter of a rectangle $= 2l + 2w$

$$
\begin{aligned}
\text{Substituting: Perimeter} &= 2(8) + 2(4) \\
&= 16 + 8 \\
&= 24\,\text{ft}
\end{aligned}
$$

The side of a square whose perimeter is 24 ft. is 6 ft.

The area of a square whose side is 6 ft. = 36 sq. ft.

24. The correct answer is K. Any point on the surface rotates once each day relative to a point in space. Each revolution is an angle of 360°. In two days, two revolutions take place, $360° \times 2 = 720°$.

25. The correct answer is B. $\dfrac{3}{7}, \dfrac{15}{32}$, and $\dfrac{11}{23}$ are all less than $\dfrac{1}{2}$; $\dfrac{9}{16}$ is larger than $\dfrac{1}{2}$.

Compare the size of fractions this way.

$$\frac{3}{7} \boxtimes \frac{15}{32}$$

Because the product of 7 and 15 is larger than the product of 32 and 3, $\dfrac{15}{32}$ will be found to be larger. Using the same method, $\dfrac{5}{32} < \dfrac{11}{23}$.

26. The correct answer is G. Use the Pythagorean theorem, $c^2 = a^2 + b^2$, to find the length of the diagonal:

$$c^2 = 1^2 + 1^2$$

$$c^2 = 2$$

$$c = \sqrt{2}$$

ANSWER SHEET PRACTICE TEST 10
Part I: Verbal

Scrambled Paragraphs

Paragraph 1

The second sentence is Ⓠ Ⓡ Ⓢ Ⓣ Ⓤ

The third sentence is Ⓠ Ⓡ Ⓢ Ⓣ Ⓤ

The fourth sentence is Ⓠ Ⓡ Ⓢ Ⓣ Ⓤ

The fifth sentence is Ⓠ Ⓡ Ⓢ Ⓣ Ⓤ

The sixth sentence is Ⓠ Ⓡ Ⓢ Ⓣ Ⓤ

Paragraph 2

The second sentence is Ⓠ Ⓡ Ⓢ Ⓣ Ⓤ

The third sentence is Ⓠ Ⓡ Ⓢ Ⓣ Ⓤ

The fourth sentence is Ⓠ Ⓡ Ⓢ Ⓣ Ⓤ

The fifth sentence is Ⓠ Ⓡ Ⓢ Ⓣ Ⓤ

The sixth sentence is Ⓠ Ⓡ Ⓢ Ⓣ Ⓤ

Logical Reasoning

3. Ⓐ Ⓑ Ⓒ Ⓓ Ⓔ

4. Ⓕ Ⓖ Ⓗ Ⓙ Ⓚ

5. Ⓐ Ⓑ Ⓒ Ⓓ Ⓔ

Reading

6. Ⓕ Ⓖ Ⓗ Ⓙ Ⓚ

7. Ⓐ Ⓑ Ⓒ Ⓓ Ⓔ

8. Ⓕ Ⓖ Ⓗ Ⓙ Ⓚ

9. Ⓐ Ⓑ Ⓒ Ⓓ Ⓔ

10. Ⓕ Ⓖ Ⓗ Ⓙ Ⓚ

11. Ⓐ Ⓑ Ⓒ Ⓓ Ⓔ

12. Ⓕ Ⓖ Ⓗ Ⓙ Ⓚ

13. Ⓐ Ⓑ Ⓒ Ⓓ Ⓔ

PART II: MATHEMATICS
PROBLEM SOLVING

14. Ⓕ Ⓖ Ⓗ Ⓙ Ⓚ

15. Ⓐ Ⓑ Ⓒ Ⓓ Ⓔ

16. Ⓕ Ⓖ Ⓗ Ⓙ Ⓚ

17. Ⓐ Ⓑ Ⓒ Ⓓ Ⓔ

18. Ⓕ Ⓖ Ⓗ Ⓙ Ⓚ

19. Ⓐ Ⓑ Ⓒ Ⓓ Ⓔ

20. Ⓕ Ⓖ Ⓗ Ⓙ Ⓚ

21. Ⓐ Ⓑ Ⓒ Ⓓ Ⓔ

22. Ⓕ Ⓖ Ⓗ Ⓙ Ⓚ

23. Ⓐ Ⓑ Ⓒ Ⓓ Ⓔ

24. Ⓕ Ⓖ Ⓗ Ⓙ Ⓚ

25. Ⓐ Ⓑ Ⓒ Ⓓ Ⓔ

26. Ⓕ Ⓖ Ⓗ Ⓙ Ⓚ

answer sheet

Practice Test 10

PART 1: VERBAL

13 Questions • 20 Minutes

QUESTIONS 1-2: SCRAMBLED PARAGRAPHS

Directions: The paragraph below consists of six sentences in scrambled order. The first, or topic, sentence is given, and you are to arrange the rest in an order that makes sense, each sentence following from the one before in that it explains the earlier one or adds to it.

Write the numbers to the left of the letters (in pencil so you can change them as often as you need). When you are satisfied, mark your choices on the answer sheet.

Because you get no partial credit for having only some of the sentences in a paragraph in order and because trying different arrangements to find which reads best requires more time than other test questions, each of the scrambled paragraphs carries twice the weight of other questions on the test.

1. Probably until as late as the 1960s, Americans thought of the USA as a melting pot: a place where many cultures were blended into one.

   _____**Q.** If the trend continues, we may well all end up hyphenating ourselves: Bulgarian-American, Scottish-American, Fijian-American, etc.

   _____**R.** Most of the early immigrants immediately Americanized their names, learned English as rapidly as possible, and quickly adopted the prevailing culture as they saw it.

   _____**S.** Might it not be better all around to turn back the trend to restore the balance between our national oneness and our own separateness?

   _____**T.** We will eat the dishes of our long-ago ancestors, perhaps dress like them, speak only their language, and have as our school major, say, Fijian studies.

   _____**U.** But increasingly since the sixties, the one-time virtue of assimilation has been replaced by an insistence on one's own particular ethnicity, no matter how distant the source.

The second sentence is   Ⓠ Ⓡ Ⓢ Ⓣ Ⓤ
The third sentence is   Ⓠ Ⓡ Ⓢ Ⓣ Ⓤ
The fourth sentence is   Ⓠ Ⓡ Ⓢ Ⓣ Ⓤ
The fifth sentence is   Ⓠ Ⓡ Ⓢ Ⓣ Ⓤ
The sixth sentence is   Ⓠ Ⓡ Ⓢ Ⓣ Ⓤ

155

2. Most of the medicines we rely on today have their source in plants used through the ages because they produced or seemed to produce cures.

_____Q. Modern medicine, however, has managed to locate the salient ingredient in most of them, many of which have become pharmacological standbys.

_____R. Scientists have more recently discovered that the purple coneflower, used by the Plains Indians to treat infectious disease, contains active substances with antibiotic, antiinflammatory, and immunostimulatory effects.

_____S. Think of the possible lifesaving cures being lost to us forever through the ongoing destruction of the world's tropical rainforests, where many of today's medicines were first discovered.

_____T. For example, ephedrine, used to dilate constricted bronchial tubes, comes from the plant Ephedra Sinical, used five thousand years ago by the Chinese to treat asthma.

_____U. The doctors, witch doctors, shamans, and ordinary people who depended upon these plants and herbs had no idea what the effective ingredient was.

The second sentence is Ⓠ Ⓡ Ⓢ Ⓣ Ⓤ
The third sentence is Ⓠ Ⓡ Ⓢ Ⓣ Ⓤ
The fourth sentence is Ⓠ Ⓡ Ⓢ Ⓣ Ⓤ
The fifth sentence is Ⓠ Ⓡ Ⓢ Ⓣ Ⓤ
The sixth sentence is Ⓠ Ⓡ Ⓢ Ⓣ Ⓤ

QUESTIONS 3–5: LOGICAL REASONING

Directions: Read each question very carefully and choose the **best** answer from the five choices given. Select your answer based **only** on the information provided.

3. Git's feet are green and Cled's feet are blue, but opposite when they're at the zoo. Bor's feet are gray but sometimes white, but never white when her clothes are tight. Ank's turn pink though they're usually red, but never red when she's near Cled. Bor weighs ninety, Ank much less, but today Bor's wearing Ank's dress. At the zoo today they all meet. What will be the colors of their feet?

	ANK	GIT	CLED	BOR
A.	pink	green	green	gray
B.	red	blue	blue	white
C.	red	blue	green	gray
D.	red	blue	green	white
E.	pink	blue	green	gray

4. In a certain language that uses a different word order than English, "Bring book here" is *koo soo moo*. "Stand here now" is *soo joo boo*, and "Do not bring Tomas" is *koo loo noo* Tomas. Which of the following means "Stand book here"?

F. *boo joo koo*

G. *koo boo soo*

H. *noo soo boo*

J. *boo moo soo*

K. *moo soo loo*

The problem below involves a code where, (1) each letter of the alphabet used represents a specific word no matter how often the word is used; (2) the plural and singular of a word is represented by the same letter; (3) the letter representing a word may or may not be directly above the word.

(1) *s*   *i*   *u*   *m*   *o*   *e*   means

  Far   apart   are   tooth   and   toe.

(2) *d*   *y*   *p*   *q*   *e*   means

Distant   the   eye   and   thigh.

(3) *i*   *d*   *f*   *q*   *e*   means

Close   the   teeth   and   eyes.

(4) *a*   *x*   *s*   *i*   *e*   means

Closest   are   teeth   and   tongue.

5. Which letter represents the word *teeth*?

A. *a*

B. *s*

C. *x*

D. *i*

E. *e*

QUESTIONS 6–13: READING PASSAGES

Directions: Read each passage below and answer the questions that follow. Remember to **use only the information you have read in the passage** when answering the questions; you may reread the passage if necessary.

Who is to blame for the high insurance premiums American doctors have to pay to protect themselves in case a patient sues them for "malpractice"—
5 mistreatment, either deliberate or arising from lack of knowledge and skill?

Whom you fault depends upon whether you are a doctor, an insurance executive, a malpractice attorney, or a
10 patient.

Let's start with the patient: you and me. The doctor's high insurance premiums, for some specialties as high as $100,000 a year, lead him (or her) to
15 charge more for his services. Because they must pay doctors more, health insurers

raise our premiums. Even though it costs us more because the malpractice insurance costs the doctor so much, we
20 want to be compensated if our physician goofs in treating us. So we tend to blame everybody concerned without understanding what is involved.

Doctors, many of them so discouraged
25 by the high insurance premiums that they look for other careers, blame lawyers and their greedy clients—us, the patients. Lawyers, some of whom specialize in malpractice suits and take a third or more
30 of the money awarded their clients, have no allies in this mess; everyone blames them. They in turn blame incompetent

doctors who cover for each other and "bury their mistakes."

35   Everybody blames to some degree the insurance companies that make big money from the large premiums, but the companies blame a lawsuit-crazy public, the economy which no longer makes
40   possible big gains from the money they invest, and bad doctors who create the problem.

6. This passage deals mainly with:

    F. Who is to blame for the high cost of health insurance depends upon who's placing the blame

    G. How to solve the high cost of health care by studying the problem from all aspects

    H. Health insurance: good or bad?

    J. The trouble with doctors

    K. Doctors vs. lawyers

7. From this passage we learn that

    A. the insurance companies are to blame for the health-care crisis.

    B. if someone dies, the doctor can be sued.

    C. no one blames the lawyers.

    D. patients don't want doctors to carry insurance.

    E. insurance companies no longer make high interest on the money they invest.

8. Where malpractice is concerned, lawyers

    F. remain uninvolved.

    G. are concerned with everyone's well-being.

    H. blame bad doctors.

    J. can make big money.

    K. just obey the law.

9. Who is the guilty party in this passage?

    A. The greedy client who sues

    B. The doctor who practices bad medicine

    C. The insurance company that charges exorbitant premiums

    D. The lawyer who collects exorbitant fees

    E. All of the above

Red China's tough and murderous leader, Chairman Mao Zedong, died in 1976, and his wife, Jiang Qing, was arrested and incarcerated for the part
5   she played in the infamous rule of the Gang of Four. While most Chinese people and the rest of the world were hardly sorry to see Mao go, his replacement, Deng Xiaoping, was in a quandary.
10   If he went all out in deglorifying Mao, as Khrushchev had with Stalin after the latter's death, it was possible it would weaken the power of the Communist Party, thereby interfering with
15   Deng's own plan for the march of Chinese capitalism.

So he compromised by retaining some of the Chairman's totems: the posters and portraits, the books of
20   quotations, even Mao's corpse in its sarcophagus, while he slowly set about undoing Mao's political stands. Little by little, the Chinese people unloaded the Mao books, busts, buttons, and so on,
25   until those that remained were mostly relegated to curio shops, where tourists bought them as souvenirs.

But then a strange thing happened. Each time there were student protests
30   from the mid-eighties on, including the massacre in Tiananmen Square, or there was a power struggle within the party, there would be a resurgence of Maoism. At first it was initiated by threatened
35   party leaders, but surprisingly the people themselves picked up on it. Now travelers to China find markets filled with Mao mementos: piles of badges,

torn posters, embroidered Mao portraits,
40 busts, even alarm clocks decorated with
Red Guards holding Red Bibles.

Now that Mao is dead, there is a
tendency to make of him a divinity, and
superstitious Chinese think his images
45 can protect them from harm. Old-time
Maoists even view this Mao resurgence
as a Second Coming. Foreign analysts
suspect it indicates dissatisfaction with
the present political system: discredited
50 leaders, rising crime and poverty, continuing oppression.

Meanwhile avant-garde musicians
and artists, many of them exiled during
Mao's regime, are featuring his name
55 and image in disco songs and irreverent
paintings, causing the old hardliners to
cry into their rice bowls.

It is just possible that using Mao
for pop-culture purposes is a subtle and
60 reasonably safe form of dissent, and the
beginning of the end of the last major
Communist power.

10. Which of the following best tells what this
passage is about?

   F. What China is like today

   G. How capitalism in China is working

   H. The difficulty in rekindling Mao's
ideas

   J. The return of Mao culture and
mementos

   K. How Deng Xiaoping dealt with
Communism

11. When Mao died, the Chinese people as a
whole

   A. glorified him and put his wife in
jail.

   B. were indifferent to his passing.

   C. voted Deng Xiaoping into office.

   D. set out to make a god of him.

   E. wanted to return to capitalism.

12. The passage suggests that Deng Xiaoping
did not want to

   F. do to Mao what Khrushchev had
done to Stalin.

   G. erase what was called Mao-think.

   H. have Mao's wife arrested.

   J. change the way Mao governed.

   K. retain Mao's portraits and posters
and other artifacts.

13. Which of the following explanations ac-
count for the return of Mao culture and
artifacts to present-day China?

   A. The Chinese people are so unhappy
with how things are now that Mao
looks better than he did.

   B. There's money in it for them.

   C. They think that now that he is dead
he is a deity.

   D. They are making fun of him.

   E. All of the above

PART II: MATHEMATICS
13 Questions • 20 Minutes

The following information is provided for your reference. It will likely not appear in the actual test booklet. You should memorize these formulas and symbols.

FORMULAS

- Area of a circle (with radius r) = πr^2

- Circumference of a circle = $2\pi r$

- Area of a parallelogram (with base b and height h) = bh

- Area of a trapezoid (with parallel sides a and b and height h) = $\frac{1}{2}(a+b)h$

- Volume of a cone or pyramid (with base area b and height h) = $\frac{1}{3}bh$

- Volume of a cylinder (with base area b and height h) = bh

- Volume of a sphere $\left(\text{with radius } r\right)$ = $\frac{4}{3}\pi r^3$

- Sum of the measures of the angles of a triangle = $180°$

- Area of a triangle:

  Area = $\dfrac{bh}{2}$

- For a right triangle:

  $c^2 = a^2 + b^2$

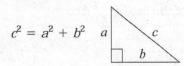

DEFINITIONS OF SYMBOLS

=   is equal to

≠   is unequal to

<   is less than

>   is greater than

≤   is less than or equal to

≥   is greater than or equal to

⊥   is perpendicular to

|| is parallel to

∠   angle

∟   right angle

⇉   parallel lines

NOTES

- Figures may not be drawn to scale. Do not assume any relationship in a diagram unless it is specifically stated or can be figured out from given information.

- Assume that a diagram is in one plane unless the problem specifically states that it is not.

- Reduce all fractions to lowest terms.

QUESTIONS 14–26: PROBLEM SOLVING

Directions: For each question, solve the problem and select the best answer from the choices given.

14. If jelly beans cost $1.60 per pound, and there are 7 jelly beans in an ounce, how much would 35 jelly beans cost?

F. $4.57

G. 50¢

H. 22.86¢

J. 245¢

K. 56¢

15. Separate 160 into 2 parts so the larger exceeds the smaller by 30. The smaller number is

A. 60

B. 80

C. 65

D. 55

E. 75

16.

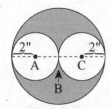

The two small circles have centers at A and C, and they touch at B, the center of the large circle. The radius of each small circle is 2 inches. The area of the shaded region is closest to: (use $\pi = 3.14$)

F. 22 sq. in.

G. 23 sq. in.

H. 24 sq. in.

J. 25 sq. in.

K. 26 sq. in.

17. A tree casts a shadow 36 feet long; at the same time, a 5-foot pole casts a 3-foot shadow. To find the height of the tree, which of the following would be used?

A. $36 \times 5 \times 3$

B. $36 \times 5 \div 3$

C. $36 \times 3 \div 5$

D. $36 \times 3 + 5$

E. $36 + 5 \times 3$

18. If $\frac{11}{16}$ lies halfway between $\frac{5}{8}$ and x, find x.

F. $\frac{2}{16}$

G. $\frac{1}{2}$

H. $\frac{3}{4}$

J. 1.1

K. $\frac{9}{16}$

19. An angle measures 40°. How much larger is its supplement than its complement?

A. 50°

B. 140°

C. 130°

D. 220°

E. 90°

20. The positive solution of the equation $5x^2 + 2 = \dfrac{14}{5}$ is $x =$

  F. $\dfrac{2}{5}$

  G. $\sqrt{\dfrac{14}{5}}$

  H. $\dfrac{16}{225}$

  J. $\sqrt{\dfrac{24}{25}}$

  K. $\dfrac{4}{5}$

21. The ratio of 2.2 hours to 10 minutes is

  F. $\dfrac{22}{1}$

  G. $\dfrac{66}{5}$

  H. $\dfrac{1}{22}$

  J. $\dfrac{5}{66}$

  K. $\dfrac{66}{1}$

22. On a chart, one figure represents 500 men. If there are four figures already, how many more would be needed to represent 4500 men?

  F. 5

  G. 9

  H. 4500

  J. 4496

  K. 2500

23. The points A, B, and C lie on a line (not necessarily in that order). If AB = 3 cm and BC = 8 cm, then which of the following *must* be true?

  A. AC = 11 cm

  B. AC = 5 cm

  C. B lies between A and C.

  D. A lies between B and C.

  E. C does not lie between A and B.

24. A photograph measuring 5" wide × 7" long must be reduced in size to fit a space 4" long in an advertising brochure. How wide must the space be so that the picture remains in proportion?

  F. $1\dfrac{4}{7}''$

  G. $2\dfrac{6}{7}''$

  H. $4\dfrac{3}{5}''$

  J. $5\dfrac{3}{5}''$

  K. $8\dfrac{3}{4}''$

25.

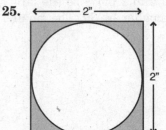

The total area of the shaded part of the figure is

  A. $\dfrac{2}{7}$ in.^{2}

  B. $\dfrac{1}{2}$ in.^{2}

  C. $\dfrac{6}{7}$ in.^{2}

  D. $1\dfrac{3}{7}$ in.^{2}

  E. $2\dfrac{1}{2}$ in.^{2}

26. A certain population of microbes grows according to the formula $P = 2^n$, where P is the size of the population and n is the number of times the population reproduces itself. If each microbe reproduces itself every 20 minutes, how large would a population of only one microbe become after 4 hours?

  F. 16

  G. 64

  H. 128

  J. 1028

  K. 4096

ANSWER KEY AND EXPLANATIONS

1. RUQTS	7. E	12. F	17. B	22. F
2. UQTRS	8. H	13. E	18. H	23. E
3. E	9. E	14. G	19. E	24. G
4. J	10. J	15. C	20. F	25. C
5. D	11. B	16. J	21. B	26. K
6. F				

PART I: VERBAL
SCRAMBLED PARAGRAPHS

1. **The correct order is RUQTS.** R is the second sentence because it describes how the "melting pot" of the topic sentence actually worked. U is third because it refers to the "one-time virtue of assimilation" already mentioned in the previous sentence. Q is fourth because it refers to the trend mentioned in the third sentence and imagines where it might go. T is fifth because it continues the behavior imagined in the previous sentence. S is sixth because it concludes by making a point about all of the above.

2. **The correct order is UQTRS.** U is the second sentence because it tells how plants mentioned in the topic sentence were used. Q is third because it tells what modern medicine did differently. T is fourth because it starts with "for example," an example of the sentence preceding. R is fifth because the "more recently" refers to the example in the third sentence. S is sixth because it concludes the topic with the need not to destroy these plants.

LOGICAL REASONING

3. **The correct answer is E.** List each name and each individual's possible feet colors (see below). The sentence about Bor and Ank tells you that Bor is wearing tight clothes, so today her feet are gray. "At the zoo" tells Cled's and Git's colors. "They all meet" means Ank will be near Cled, so her feet will be pink.

	ANK	GIT	CLED	BOR
	red	green	blue	gray (tight clothes)
	pink (near Cled)	blue (at zoo)	green (at zoo)	white
Answer:	pink	blue	green	gray

4. **The correct answer is J.** Set the given information step by step:

   1. "Bring the book here" = *koo soo moo*

   2. "Stand *here* now" = *soo joo boo*

      ("Here" must be *soo*, which is the only common word.)

   3. "Do not bring Tomas" = *koo joo noo* Tomas

      (Bring is in the first and third sentences, and so is *koo*. *Koo* means "bring.")

   Since the only word left in the first sentence is *moo*, it must mean "book."

   Putting all this together, you have "Stand book here" = _____ *moo soo*. The word stand is in sentence two, and it must be either *joo* or *boo*. So "Stand book here" is either *joo moo soo* or *boo moo soo*; the order is not important.

   The only one of these answers in the five choices given is *boo moo soo*.

5. **The correct answer is D.** To solve this problem you need to look to see what letter corresponds to the word *teeth*, by examining the 4 sentences for the word *teeth* and applying the rule that states that the plural and singular of a word are representd by the same letter. Therefore, be aware that the word *teeth* in sentence 1 is represented by the same letter representing teeth in sentences 3 and 4. Now look for a letter that appears in sentences 1, 3, and 4; the only letter that only appears in sentences 1, 3, and 4 is *i*. This must be the answer.

READING PASSAGES

6. **The correct answer is F.** This passage is about who blames who [Choice F], not merely about choice K, nor about choices J or H. It offers no opinion about choice G.

7. **The correct answer is E.** The only one of the facts given in this question that is stated as such in the passage is choice E. The first sounds right, but is only one opinion. Choices B and D may be true, but are not mentioned, and everyone blames the lawyers, choice C.

8. **The correct answer is H.** Lawyers blame doctors who bury their mistakes as stated in paragraph four. Choice J is a possibility, since it can be deduced that lawyers who take one third of the award make big money, but it is not as clearly stated as choice H. The other three choices are all wrong.

9. **The correct answer is E.** This is easy if you pick up what is being implied in the passage. All of the answers are correct.

10. **The correct answer is J.** From beginning to end, the passage deals with Mao Zedong and the lasting effect he has had on China. Choice F looks possible, but when you think about it, you see that it is just too broad a statement. The other answers are quite far from describing what the passage is about.

11. **The correct answer is B.** This is a very direct question, and the answer is found in the first paragraph. Although choices A, D, and E are untrue, choice C upon first thought seems true, but there is nothing in the passage that says Deng Xiaoping was voted into office.

12. **The correct answer is F.** The second paragraph is the key to this question as it explains Deng's thoughts on the Khrushchev-Stalin historical incident. He did not want to deglorify Mao totally. Choice J takes some thought, but Deng did want to change the way Mao governed as stated in paragraph three, where it mentions changing Mao's political stands. The other choices are false interpretations of the passage or not there at all.

13. **The correct answer is E.** Each choice—A through D—is a true interpretation or rephrasing of what is stated in the passage in the last four paragraphs.

Part II: Mathematics

PROBLEM SOLVING

14. The correct answer is G. 35 jelly beans will weigh 5 ounces, since 7 jelly beans weigh 1 ounce. Use a proportion: $\dfrac{5}{16} = \dfrac{x}{1.60}$

The cross-products are equal:

$16x = 5 \times 1.60$

$16x = 8$

or $16)\overline{\$1.60}^{\ \$.10} = 10\cancel{c}$ per ounce

5 oz cost 50¢

$\dfrac{\cancel{16}^{1}x}{\cancel{16}_{1}} = \dfrac{\cancel{8}^{1}}{\cancel{16}_{2}}; x = \dfrac{1}{2}$

$\dfrac{1}{2}$ dollar $= 50¢$

15. The correct answer is C. Let x = the smaller number

$x + 30$ = the larger number

$2x + 30 = 160$

$\underline{\quad -30 = -30 \quad}$

$\quad 2x = 130$

$\quad\ x = 65$

16. The correct answer is J.

Area of shaded portion = Area of large circle – Area of 2 small circles

$= \pi \times 4^2 - \left(\pi \times 2^2 + \pi \times 2^2\right)$

$= \pi \times 16 - \left(\pi \times 4 + \pi \times 4\right)$

$= 16\pi - 8\pi$

$= 8\pi = (8)(3.14) = 25.12$

17. The correct answer is B. $\dfrac{x\,(\text{height of tree})}{36'} = \dfrac{5'\,(\text{height of pole})}{3'\,(\text{shadow of pole})}$

$3x = 36 \times 5$

$x = 36 \times 5 \div 3$

18. The correct answer is H. Find the difference between $\frac{11}{16}$ and $\frac{5}{8}$:

$$\frac{11}{16} = \frac{11}{16}$$
$$-\frac{5}{8} = \frac{-10}{16}$$
$$\frac{1}{16}$$

Therefore, since $\frac{11}{16}$ is the middle, the other number must be $\frac{1}{16}$ greater:

$$\frac{11}{16} + \frac{1}{16} = \frac{12}{16} \text{ or } \frac{3}{4}$$

19. The correct answer is E. A 40° angle has a supplement of 140° and a complement of 50°. The difference between 140° and 50° is 90°.

20. The correct answer is F.

$$5x^2 + 2 = \frac{14}{5}$$
$$5x^2 = \frac{14}{5} - 2$$
$$5x^2 = \frac{14}{5} - \frac{10}{5}$$
$$5x^2 = \frac{4}{5}$$
$$x^2 = \frac{4}{25}$$
$$x = \frac{2}{5}$$

21. The correct answer is B.

2.2 hrs. = 2 hrs. + 0.2 hrs. (0.2 × 12.0 min.) = 120 min. + 12 min. = 132 min.

Thus, the ratio is $\frac{132 \text{ min.}}{10 \text{ min.}} = \frac{66}{6}$

22. The correct answer is F.

$$\frac{1}{500} = \frac{x}{4500}, \text{ or } 500x = 4500; x = 9$$

If 9 figures are needed in all, and there are 4 already, then 5 more are needed.

23. The correct answer is E. The three points can be analyzed like this:

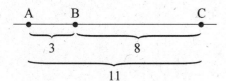

or like this:

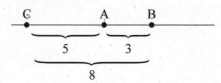

The only answer that *must* be true is choice E.

24. The correct answer is G. This is a simple proportion: $\frac{7}{4} = \frac{5}{x}$. x is the unknown width. Cross-multiply:

$7x = 20$

$x = \frac{20}{7}$, or $2\frac{6}{7}''$

25. The correct answer is C. Subtract the area of the circle from the area of the square to find the area of just the shaded part.

Note that the diameter of the circle equals the width of the square.

Area of square = s^2 = 4 sq. in.

Area of circle = $\pi r^2 = \pi(1)^2 = \pi$ sq. in.

Area of square – Area of circle

$= 4 \text{ sq. in.} - \frac{22}{7} \text{ sq. in.}$

$= \frac{6}{7} \text{ sq. in., or } \frac{6}{7} \text{ in.}^2$

26. The correct answer is K. The population would reproduce 12 times in 4 hours. The size then is $P = 2^{12}$

$= 2 \cdot 2 \cdot 2 \cdot 2 \cdot 2 \cdot 2 \cdot 2 \cdot 2 \cdot 2 \cdot 2 \cdot 2 \cdot 2 = 4096$

answers practice test 10

APPENDIX

The Hunter College High School
Entrance Examination

Practice Test 1

Practice Test 2

The Hunter College High School Entrance Examination

The Hunter College High School Entrance Examination is offered in January to all sixth-grade students residing within the five boroughs of New York City who meet specific criteria in reading and mathematics.

At present, the standardized test score criterion is the 90th national percentile (715 Scaled Score on CTB) or higher in Total Reading and at the 90th national percentile (724 Scaled Score on CTB) or higher in Total Mathematics in order to be permitted to take the entrance exam.

The Hunter College High School Entrance Examination is 3 hours long and consists of approximately 100 multiple-choice questions in reading comprehension, vocabulary, sentence completion, grammar, and mathematics. The final part of the exam consists of an essay to be written on an assigned topic.

The passing score for the exam varies from year to year, depending on the number of students who apply and the actual number of students the school can accept.

The essay is read only if the student has met the passing grade for the multiple-choice part of the test. If the essay is of acceptable quality, the student has passed the exam—e.g., if the cutoff was 86, a student who scores an 88 might be accepted over a student who scored 90 if the quality and content of the essay are better.

DIRECTIONS FOR TAKING THE PRACTICE TESTS

The tests that follow are patterned on the Hunter College High School Entrance Examination. The multiple-choice questions (parts I through V) are designed to be taken in 30 minutes. The essay question (part VI) should be taken separately in 30 minutes.

The breakdown of the practice tests with the suggested time allotments is as follows:

Part I, Questions 1–10, Vocabulary	6 minutes
Part II, Questions 11–13, Sentence Completion	2 minutes
Part III, Questions 14–16, Grammar	2 minutes
Part IV, Questions 17–24, Reading Comprehension	8 minutes
Part V, Questions 25–36, Mathematics	12 minutes
Part VI, Essay Question	30 minutes

ANSWER SHEET PRACTICE TEST 1

Part I: Vocabulary

1. Ⓐ Ⓑ Ⓒ Ⓓ Ⓔ   4. Ⓐ Ⓑ Ⓒ Ⓓ Ⓔ   7. Ⓐ Ⓑ Ⓒ Ⓓ Ⓔ   9. Ⓐ Ⓑ Ⓒ Ⓓ Ⓔ
2. Ⓐ Ⓑ Ⓒ Ⓓ Ⓔ   5. Ⓐ Ⓑ Ⓒ Ⓓ Ⓔ   8. Ⓐ Ⓑ Ⓒ Ⓓ Ⓔ   10. Ⓐ Ⓑ Ⓒ Ⓓ Ⓔ
3. Ⓐ Ⓑ Ⓒ Ⓓ Ⓔ   6. Ⓐ Ⓑ Ⓒ Ⓓ Ⓔ

Part II: Sentence Completion

11. Ⓐ Ⓑ Ⓒ Ⓓ Ⓔ   12. Ⓐ Ⓑ Ⓒ Ⓓ Ⓔ   13. Ⓐ Ⓑ Ⓒ Ⓓ Ⓔ

Part III: Grammar

14. Ⓐ Ⓑ Ⓒ Ⓓ Ⓔ   15. Ⓐ Ⓑ Ⓒ Ⓓ Ⓔ   16. Ⓐ Ⓑ Ⓒ Ⓓ Ⓔ

Part iV: Reading Comprehension

17. Ⓐ Ⓑ Ⓒ Ⓓ Ⓔ   19. Ⓐ Ⓑ Ⓒ Ⓓ Ⓔ   21. Ⓐ Ⓑ Ⓒ Ⓓ Ⓔ   23. Ⓐ Ⓑ Ⓒ Ⓓ Ⓔ
18. Ⓐ Ⓑ Ⓒ Ⓓ Ⓔ   20. Ⓐ Ⓑ Ⓒ Ⓓ Ⓔ   22. Ⓐ Ⓑ Ⓒ Ⓓ Ⓔ   24. Ⓐ Ⓑ Ⓒ Ⓓ Ⓔ

Part V: Mathematics

25. Ⓐ Ⓑ Ⓒ Ⓓ Ⓔ   28. Ⓐ Ⓑ Ⓒ Ⓓ Ⓔ   31. Ⓐ Ⓑ Ⓒ Ⓓ Ⓔ   34. Ⓐ Ⓑ Ⓒ Ⓓ Ⓔ
26. Ⓐ Ⓑ Ⓒ Ⓓ Ⓔ   29. Ⓐ Ⓑ Ⓒ Ⓓ Ⓔ   32. Ⓐ Ⓑ Ⓒ Ⓓ Ⓔ   35. Ⓐ Ⓑ Ⓒ Ⓓ Ⓔ
27. Ⓐ Ⓑ Ⓒ Ⓓ Ⓔ   30. Ⓐ Ⓑ Ⓒ Ⓓ Ⓔ   33. Ⓐ Ⓑ Ⓒ Ⓓ Ⓔ   36. Ⓐ Ⓑ Ⓒ Ⓓ Ⓔ

answer sheet

Practice Test 1

PART 1: VOCABULARY

10 Questions • 6 Minutes

FOR QUESTIONS 1–10, CHOOSE THE WORD OR PHRASE THAT MEANS THE SAME, OR MOST NEARLY THE SAME, AS THE CAPITALIZED WORD.

Directions: Choose the best answer for each question and mark your choice on the Answer Sheet for Practice Test 1. Correct answers and explanations follow the test.

1. EXONERATE
   - (A) vindicate
   - (B) condemn
   - (C) exalt
   - (D) display
   - (E) expel

2. CONDIMENT
   - (A) seasoning
   - (B) allergy
   - (C) sloppy
   - (D) condition
   - (E) cornerstone

3. PLATITUDE
   - (A) plateau
   - (B) duck
   - (C) exciting
   - (D) cliché
   - (E) altitude

4. LEXICON
   - (A) elf
   - (B) train
   - (C) dictionary
   - (D) pulpit
   - (E) mammal

5. QUIVER
   - (A) shout
   - (B) tremble
   - (C) slice
   - (D) cease
   - (E) holster

6. IMMINENT
   - (A) existing
   - (B) innate
   - (C) important
   - (D) impending
   - (E) exciting

7. DUPLICITY
   - (A) honest
   - (B) durability
   - (C) truth
   - (D) endurance
   - (E) deception

8. OBLIVIOUS
   - (A) cruel
   - (B) forgetful
   - (C) lovable
   - (D) concerned
   - (E) fretful

9. DEITY

   (A) mankind

   (B) demon

   (C) divinity

   (D) head table

   (E) destiny

10. CONFORMITY

   (A) agreement

   (B) shape

   (C) difference

   (D) ignorance

   (E) structure

PART II: SENTENCE COMPLETION

3 Questions • 2 Minutes

FOR QUESTIONS 11–13, SELECT THE WORD THAT BEST COMPLETES THE SENTENCE GIVEN.

11. He was _____ when his new bike was stolen.

   (A) happy

   (B) drab

   (C) furious

   (D) indifferent

   (E) None of the above

12. I have to _____ our plans for this evening.

   (A) launder

   (B) research

   (C) cancel

   (D) squander

   (E) None of the above

13. The _____ for the best candidate went on for months.

   (A) quest

   (B) vacation

   (C) tour

   (D) reaction

   (E) None of the above

PART III: GRAMMAR

3 Questions • 2 Minutes

SOME OF THE FOLLOWING SENTENCES CONTAIN ERRORS IN GRAMMAR, SPELLING, OR PUNCTUATION. IF THERE IS AN ERROR, MARK YOUR ANSWER SHEET FOR THE LETTER OF THE UNDERLINED PORTION THAT MUST BE CHANGED TO MAKE THE SENTENCE CORRECT. THERE IS NO ERROR IN A SENTENCE, CHOOSE E. NONE OF THESE. NO SENTENCE CONTAINS MORE THAN ONE ERROR.

14. She <u>wanted</u> to borrow <u>Johns'</u> book
      (A)   **(B)**
but <u>decided</u> to <u>purchase</u> her own.
     (C)   **(D)**
<u>None of these</u>.
   (E)

15. Sam will enter the <u>writing</u> contest or
              (A)
<u>devote</u> his <u>available</u> time to <u>delivering</u>
 (B)   **(C)**   **(D)**
newspapers. <u>None of these</u>.
        (E)

16. The <u>paragraph</u> told about
      (A)
<u>Thomas Edison</u> and the <u>discovery</u>
    (B)   **(C)**
of the <u>light</u> bulb. <u>None of these</u>.
     (E)   **(D)**

PART IV: READING COMPREHENSION

8 Questions • 8 Minutes

READ EACH PASSAGE CAREFULLY. THEN, ON THE BASIS OF WHAT YOU HAVE READ, DECIDE WHICH OF THE POSSIBLE RESPONSES IS THE BEST ANSWER TO EACH QUESTION. YOU MAY READ THE PASSAGE AGAIN IF NECESSARY.

Aerobic exercise has as its main goal the strengthening of many of the vital organs of the body. It seeks to make the heart and blood vessels resistant to what

5 physicians call cardiovascular diseases. To the layman, this translates into heart attacks and hardening of the arteries. Aerobic exercises also strengthen the lungs. They become more resistant to

10 pulmonary diseases and process more oxygen.

Together the cardiovascular and pulmonary systems supply our bodies with blood nutrients and oxygen. It seems

15 obvious that any well-supplied body organ will be a healthier organ.

The way the cardiovascular and pulmonary systems are strengthened is by stressing them in a healthful way.

20 Running is one of the ways of doing this. To run aerobically, one runs at a pace that can be maintained for a long period of time. Thirty minutes would be a minimum time. During this time,

25 a person in decent physical shape will run about 3.5 to 4 miles. When you train toward this goal, the heart beats more strongly, the lungs process more oxygen, and the arteries respond by developing

30 excellent elasticity.

A well-developed healthy cardiovascular-pulmonary system is much more important than well-developed arms and shoulders. Remember, nobody ever died

35 of weak arms.

17. This passage is mainly about

(A) running.

(B) cardiovascular and pulmonary disease.

(C) aerobic exercise.

(D) getting in shape.

(E) the benefits of stress.

18. According to the passage,

(A) aerobics will cure cardiovascular disease.

(B) the longer and faster you run, the better.

(C) oxygen supply can be improved by aerobic exercise.

(D) excess stress is beneficial.

(E) All of the above

19. Aerobic exercise

(A) benefits only certain parts of the body.

(B) can benefit just about all of the body.

(C) always involves running.

(D) is fairly easy.

(E) can cure a faulty heart.

20. Cardiovascular diseases involve

(A) the heart.

(B) the arteries.

(C) vital organs.

(D) hardening blood vessels.

(E) All of the above

Thirty states had unemployment of 10 percent or more last February, and the rate in West Virginia was at 21 percent. This is the highest rate for any

5 state since the U.S. government started recording unemployment statistics by states in the late 1960s.

The state-by-state and metropolitan employment statistics, which are not

10 adjusted for such seasonal variations as weather and school closings, showed that there were nine more states with unemployment rates of 10 percent or

more than there had been in the same
month a year earlier.
   Twenty-two of these states had
unemployment rates that reached or
exceeded the national seasonally unadjusted rate of 11.3 percent in February.
   After West Virginia, the states
with the highest unemployment rates
in February were Michigan—16.5
percent; Alabama—16.1 percent; Ohio—
14.5 percent; and Pennsylvania—14.1
percent.
   West Virginia has had great layoffs in
its coal mining industry. The other states
most severely affected are also highly
industrialized. It is heavy industry in the
United States that is suffering most in the
general unemployment across the land.

21. This passage is mainly about

   (A) heavy industry in the United
States.

   (B) unemployment and world
markets.

   (C) rates of unemployment in the
United States.

   (D) the reasons for unemployment in
the United States.

   (E) the effects of unemployment in the
United States.

22. According to this passage, West Virginia

   (A) has more people unemployed than
any other state.

   (B) had better than one out of five
employable people unemployed in
February.

   (C) has a large uneducated
population.

   (D) has no modern technology to
speak of.

   (E) always does poorly in February.

23. The most recent February figures

   (A) were seasonally adjusted.

   (B) were better in terms of unemployment in several states.

   (C) can be compared to statistics compiled over several generations.

   (D) indicate that 40 percent of the
states have unemployment below
10 percent.

   (E) indicate a severe depression
across the United States.

24. The passage indicates that

   (A) West Virginia and Michigan have
a lot of coal miners without work.

   (B) West Virginia and Michigan are
in need of new technology.

   (C) West Virginia and Michigan make
cars and trucks.

   (D) West Virginia and Michigan are
both highly industrialized.

   (E) West Virginia and Michigan are
part of Appalachia.

PART V: MATHEMATICS

12 Questions • 12 Minutes

CHOOSE THE CORRECT ANSWER FOR EACH PROBLEM.

25. Which of the following fractions is the smallest: $\frac{5}{12}, \frac{4}{9}, \frac{6}{11}, \frac{4}{7}, \frac{1}{2}$?

(A) $\frac{6}{11}$

(B) $\frac{5}{12}$

(C) $\frac{4}{9}$

(D) $\frac{4}{7}$

(E) $\frac{1}{2}$

26. A 10-minute call to Hawaii after 9 p.m. costs $5.75. If the charge for the first 3 minutes was $3.65, what was the charge for each additional minute?

(A) $21

(B) $2.10

(C) $.30

(D) $.03

(E) None of the above

27. James can ride his bicycle to school, $3\frac{1}{4}$ miles away, in 15 minutes. At the same rate, how long will it take him to ride to a town 13 miles away?

(A) $42\frac{1}{4}$ minutes

(B) $3\frac{1}{4}$ hours

(C) 1 hour

(D) $48\frac{3}{4}$ minutes

(E) None of the above

28. A scale on a map is $1\frac{1}{2}$ inches = 10 miles. How many miles does a 21-inch line represent?

(A) $31\frac{1}{2}$

(B) 140

(C) .0714

(D) 150

(E) None of the above

29. The area of a triangle with base 21 inches and height $4\frac{1}{2}$ inches is equal to

(A) $94\frac{1}{4}$ sq in

(B) $47\frac{1}{4}$ sq in

(C) $25\frac{1}{2}$ sq in

(D) 30 in

(E) None of the above

30. Mary weighs 111 pounds. She loses 4 pounds. To the nearest percent, how much has she lost?

(A) 3%

(B) $3\frac{1}{2}$%

(C) 4%

(D) .04%

(E) None of the above

31. If $5x = 10y$ and $x = 2\frac{1}{2}$, then $y =$

    (A) 5

    (B) $\frac{1}{2}$

    (C) $1\frac{1}{4}$

    (D) $12\frac{1}{2}$

    (E) None of the above

32. 432_{five} is equal to what numeral in base 10?

    (A) 210

    (B) 105

    (C) 202

    (D) 117

    (E) None of the above

33. Find the area of a circle with a radius of 14. (Use $\pi = \frac{22}{7}$.)

    (A) 616 sq in

    (B) 44 sq in

    (C) 88 in

    (D) 308 in

    (E) None of the above

34. $\frac{1}{5}\%$ of 585 is equal to

    (A) 117

    (B) .0117

    (C) .117

    (D) 1.17

    (E) None of the above

35. A coat was on sale for $83.30. This was 85% of the original price. The original price of the coat was

    (A) $100

    (B) $85

    (C) $83.30

    (D) $147

    (E) None of the above

36. The perimeter of a square is 30 inches. Its area is

    (A) 225

    (B) 22.5

    (C) 55.75

    (D) 56.25

    (E) None of the above

PART VI: ESSAY QUESTION

1 Questions • 30 Minutes

WRITE AN ESSAY ON "A MEMORABLE VACATION." DESCRIBE A RECENT VACATION (SUMMER, WINTER, FALL, OR SPRING) AND TELL WHAT MADE IT SPECIAL.

ANSWER KEY AND EXPLANATIONS

1. A	9. C	16. E	23. D	30. C
2. A	10. A	17. C	24. D	31. C
3. D	11. C	18. C	25. B	32. D
4. C	12. C	19. B	26. C	33. A
5. B	13. A	20. E	27. C	34. D
6. D	14. B	21. C	28. B	35. E
7. E	15. A	22. B	29. B	36. D
8. B				

PART I: VOCABULARY

1. **The correct answer is (A).** *Exonerate* means "to vindicate."

   The court exonerated the accused.
   The court vindicated the accused.

2. **The correct answer is (A).** *Condiment* is a food seasoning.

   Condiments do wonders for chicken.
   Seasonings do wonders for chicken.

3. **The correct answer is (D).** *Platitude* is the same as cliché.

   His speech was full of platitudes.
   His speech was full of clichés.

4. **The correct answer is (C).** A *lexicon* is a dictionary.

   Look up the words you don't know in a dictionary.
   Look up the words you don't know in a lexicon.

5. **The correct answer is (B).** To *quiver* is to tremble.

   The frightening movie made him quiver.
   The frightening movie made him tremble.

6. **The correct answer is (D).** *Imminent* means "impending."

   The results of her experimental work are imminent.
   The results of her experimental work are impending.

7. **The correct answer is (E).** *Duplicity* means "fraud" or "deception."

   That she pretended to be my friend yet spread ugly rumors about me was evidence of her duplicity.

   That she pretended to be my friend yet spread ugly rumors about me was evidence of her deception.

8. **The correct answer is (B).** *Oblivious* means "forgetful."

   She walked without an umbrella, oblivious to the rain.
   She walked without an umbrella, forgetful of the rain.

9. **The correct answer is (C).** *Deity* means "divinity."

   The Greek gods were models of deity.
   The Greek gods were models of divinity.

10. **The correct answer is (A).** *Conformity* means "agreement."

    In conformity with the rule, the meeting was adjourned.
    In agreement with the rule, the meeting was adjourned.

PART II: SENTENCE COMPLETION

11. **The correct answer is (C).** *Furious* means "full of anger."

    He was full of anger when his new bike was stolen.

12. **The correct answer is (C).** *Cancel* means "to call off."

    I have to call off our plans for this evening.

13. **The correct answer is (A).** *Quest* means "search."

    The search for the best candidate went on for a month.

PART III: GRAMMAR

14. **The correct answer is (A).** Johns' should be John's, denoting the singular possessive case.

15. **The correct answer is (A).** Writting is an incorrect spelling. It should be writing.

16. **The correct answer is (E).** This sentence is correct.

PART IV: READING COMPREHENSION

17. **The correct answer is (C).** The passage is all about aerobic exercise and its benefits.

18. **The correct answer is (C).** The passage states that aerobic exercise strengthens the lungs and allows them to process more oxygen.

19. **The correct answer is (B).** The passage infers that all of our organs benefit from aerobic exercise.

20. **The correct answer is (E).** All answers are correct.

21. **The correct answer is (C).** The passage deals mainly with percentage, i.e., rates of unemployment.

22. **The correct answer is (B).** 21% is more than $\frac{1}{5}$

23. **The correct answer is (D).** If 30 states had unemployment above 10%, then 20 states (40%) had below 10%.

24. **The correct answer is (D).** The passage states that both are industrialized.

Part V: Mathematics

25. The correct answer is B. $\frac{5}{12} = 0.42; \frac{4}{9} = 0.44; \frac{6}{11} = 0.55; \frac{4}{7} = 0.57;$ and $\frac{1}{2} = 0.50$; therefore, 0.42, or $\frac{5}{12}$, is the smallest fraction.

26. The correct answer is (C). $5.75 – $3.65 = $2.10 for 7 minutes. Therefore, $2.10 ÷ 7 = $.30.

27. The correct answer is (C). $13 \text{ miles} \div 3\frac{1}{4} = 13 \div \frac{13}{4}$, or $\frac{13}{1} \times \frac{4}{13} = 4$. Therefore, it will take 15 minutes × 4 = 60 minutes, or 1 hour, to ride 13 miles.

28. The correct answer is (B). $21 \div 1\frac{1}{2}$ is $21 \div \frac{3}{2}$, or $\frac{21}{1} \times \frac{2}{3} = 14$; therefore, a 21" line represents 14 × 10 = 140 miles.

29. The correct answer is (B). Area of a triangle $= \frac{1}{2} \times \text{base} \times \text{height}$, or
$A = \frac{1}{2} \times \frac{21}{1} \times \frac{9}{2} = \frac{189}{4}$.

$\frac{189}{4} = 47\frac{1}{4}$ square units.

30. The correct answer is (C). 4 out of $111 = \frac{4}{111}$, or 4 ÷ 111, which is:

$111\overline{)4.000}^{\,0.0360}$ = 0.04, or 4%

31. The correct answer is (C). If $5x = 10y$ and $x = 2\frac{1}{2}$, then $5 \times 2\frac{1}{2} = 10y$, or $12\frac{1}{2} = 10y$.

Therefore, dividing by 10, $y = 12\frac{1}{2} \div 10 = \frac{25}{2} \times \frac{1}{10} = \frac{25}{20} = 1\frac{5}{20} = 1\frac{1}{4}$.

32. The correct answer is (D).

$$432_{\text{five}} = \left(4 \times 5^2\right) + \left(3 \times 5\right) + \left(2 \times 1\right)$$
$$= \left(4 \times 25\right) + \left(15\right) + \left(2\right)$$
$$= 100 + 15 + 2$$
$$= 117$$

Therefore, $432_{\text{five}} = 117$.

33. The correct answer is (A). Area of a circle $= \pi r^2$; $(\pi = \frac{22}{7})$

Area $= \frac{22}{7} \times \frac{14}{1} \times \frac{14}{1}$

$\frac{22}{1} \times \frac{2}{1} \times \frac{14}{1}$

$44 \times 14 = 616$.

Therefore, the area of the circle is equal to 616 square units.

34. The correct answer is (D). $\frac{1}{5}\% = 0.2\%$, or 0.002 as a decimal. Therefore, 0.002 × 585 = 1.170, or 1.17.

35. The correct answer is (E). If \$83.30 was 85% of the original, then \$83.30 = 0.85 of x. Therefore, 83.30 ÷ 0.85 = x, or x = \$98.

36. The correct answer is (D). If the perimeter is 30 inches, then the side is $30 \div 4 = 7\frac{1}{2}$ and $A = s^2$, or $\left(7\frac{1}{2}\right)^2$. Therefore, the area is $56\frac{1}{4}$, or 56.25 square inches.

Part VI: ESSAY

An essay is a short written discussion on a particular theme or topic. There are three basic parts to a complete essay:

1. An introduction—an opening paragraph stating the theme and supporting the main idea

2. The exposition—two or three paragraphs explaining and giving examples in support of the theme

3. The conclusion—a paragraph that restates the theme and summarizes the main idea

There is no correct answer to an essay question. Teachers who are able to work with students can concentrate on teaching them how to write an essay as part of their Language Arts curriculum.

A student working on his or her own can look at the model, study its structure, and practice writing his or her own answer following the same pattern.

Remember: The essay is an important part of the exam and might mean the difference between acceptance or rejection. The following is an example of a model essay:

My Visit to San Francisco

Introduction
main idea

During my spring vacation, my family and I visited San Francisco. We stayed in a beautiful hotel overlooking the Golden Gate Bridge. This is a huge bridge spanning San Francisco Bay.

Exposition
details about
topic

Many of the streets of San Francisco are amazing because of their steepness. They twist and turn so you only hope that the brakes of the car you're in don't fail.

We took a trolley ride to Fisherman's Wharf. The variety of stores and restaurants there is bewildering. From the wharf, you can take a ferry to Alcatraz Island and see the old federal penitentiary.

The most exciting part of the trip was driving on the edge of a cliff to a mountain area called Big Sur. The scenery was breathtaking.

Conclusion
summary of
main idea

I will never forget San Francisco. My hope is to return someday. There's so much more I want to see and do that I can't wait until my family goes back again.

ANSWER SHEET PRACTICE TEST 2

Part I: Vocabulary

1. Ⓐ Ⓑ Ⓒ Ⓓ Ⓔ   4. Ⓐ Ⓑ Ⓒ Ⓓ Ⓔ   7. Ⓐ Ⓑ Ⓒ Ⓓ Ⓔ   9. Ⓐ Ⓑ Ⓒ Ⓓ Ⓔ
2. Ⓐ Ⓑ Ⓒ Ⓓ Ⓔ   5. Ⓐ Ⓑ Ⓒ Ⓓ Ⓔ   8. Ⓐ Ⓑ Ⓒ Ⓓ Ⓔ   10. Ⓐ Ⓑ Ⓒ Ⓓ Ⓔ
3. Ⓐ Ⓑ Ⓒ Ⓓ Ⓔ   6. Ⓐ Ⓑ Ⓒ Ⓓ Ⓔ

Part II: Sentence Completion

11. Ⓐ Ⓑ Ⓒ Ⓓ Ⓔ   12. Ⓐ Ⓑ Ⓒ Ⓓ Ⓔ   13. Ⓐ Ⓑ Ⓒ Ⓓ Ⓔ

Part III: Grammar

14. Ⓐ Ⓑ Ⓒ Ⓓ Ⓔ   15. Ⓐ Ⓑ Ⓒ Ⓓ Ⓔ   16. Ⓐ Ⓑ Ⓒ Ⓓ Ⓔ

Part iV: Reading Comprehension

17. Ⓐ Ⓑ Ⓒ Ⓓ Ⓔ   19. Ⓐ Ⓑ Ⓒ Ⓓ Ⓔ   21. Ⓐ Ⓑ Ⓒ Ⓓ Ⓔ   23. Ⓐ Ⓑ Ⓒ Ⓓ Ⓔ
18. Ⓐ Ⓑ Ⓒ Ⓓ Ⓔ   20. Ⓐ Ⓑ Ⓒ Ⓓ Ⓔ   22. Ⓐ Ⓑ Ⓒ Ⓓ Ⓔ   24. Ⓐ Ⓑ Ⓒ Ⓓ Ⓔ

Part V: Mathematics

25. Ⓐ Ⓑ Ⓒ Ⓓ Ⓔ   28. Ⓐ Ⓑ Ⓒ Ⓓ Ⓔ   31. Ⓐ Ⓑ Ⓒ Ⓓ Ⓔ   34. Ⓐ Ⓑ Ⓒ Ⓓ Ⓔ
26. Ⓐ Ⓑ Ⓒ Ⓓ Ⓔ   29. Ⓐ Ⓑ Ⓒ Ⓓ Ⓔ   32. Ⓐ Ⓑ Ⓒ Ⓓ Ⓔ   35. Ⓐ Ⓑ Ⓒ Ⓓ Ⓔ
27. Ⓐ Ⓑ Ⓒ Ⓓ Ⓔ   30. Ⓐ Ⓑ Ⓒ Ⓓ Ⓔ   33. Ⓐ Ⓑ Ⓒ Ⓓ Ⓔ   36. Ⓐ Ⓑ Ⓒ Ⓓ Ⓔ

answer sheet

Practice Test 2

PART 1: VOCABULARY

10 Questions • 6 Minutes

FOR QUESTIONS 1–10, CHOOSE THE WORD OR PHRASE THAT MEANS THE SAME, OR MOST NEARLY THE SAME, AS THE CAPITALIZED WORD.

Directions: Choose the best answer for each question and mark your choice on the Answer Sheet for Practice Test 2. Correct answers and explanations follow the test.

1. UNCANNY
   - (A) natural
   - (B) eerie
   - (C) canned
   - (D) true
   - (E) unclear

2. SQUANDER
   - (A) sane
   - (B) store
   - (C) increase
   - (D) waste
   - (E) squelch

3. ASSAY
   - (A) compose
   - (B) discuss
   - (C) agree
   - (D) survey
   - (E) assign

4. POPULATION
   - (A) popular
   - (B) disease
   - (C) herd
   - (D) inhabitants
   - (E) crowd

5. RESISTANCE
   - (A) opposition
   - (B) unconcern
   - (C) meeting
   - (D) powerless
   - (E) resonance

6. PLAUSIBLE
   - (A) applause
   - (B) credible
   - (C) disbelief
   - (D) pause
   - (E) pertinent

7. CURTAIL
   - (A) drape
   - (B) shorten
   - (C) lengthen
   - (D) enlarge
   - (E) create

8. MANEUVER
   - (A) artifact
   - (B) tactic
   - (C) manpower
   - (D) declare
   - (E) mannerism

9. RICKETY

    (A) strong

    (B) diseased

    (C) weak

    (D) stable

    (E) ridiculous

10. MORALITY

    (A) humble

    (B) fable

    (C) unethical

    (D) virtue

    (E) determination

PART II: SENTENCE COMPLETION

3 Questions • 2 Minutes

FOR QUESTIONS 11–13, SELECT THE WORD THAT BEST COMPLETES THE SENTENCE GIVEN.

11. My _____ response is yes before I think it through.

    (A) negative

    (B) pensive

    (C) cloudy

    (D) initial

    (E) None of the above

12. It is _____ that we discover a cure.

    (A) difficult

    (B) critical

    (C) salutary

    (D) subscript

    (E) None of the above

13. The coach explained his _____ to the team before the game.

    (A) retirement

    (B) luxury

    (C) bodice

    (D) strategy

    (E) None of the above

PART III: GRAMMAR

3 Questions • 2 Minutes

SOME OF THE FOLLOWING SENTENCES CONTAIN ERRORS IN GRAMMAR, SPELLING, OR PUNCTUATION. IF THERE IS AN ERROR, MARK YOUR ANSWER SHEET FOR THE LETTER OF THE UNDERLINED PORTION THAT MUST BE CHANGED TO MAKE THE SENTENCE CORRECT. THERE IS NO ERROR IN A SENTENCE, CHOOSE E. NONE OF THESE. NO SENTENCE CONTAINS MORE THAN ONE ERROR.

14. The <u>Smith</u> family <u>frequently</u> went
       (A)   **(B)**
<u>picnicing</u> on <u>Sundays</u>. <u>None of these</u>.
  (C)   **(D)**   **(E)**

15. <u>It's</u> a cold <u>dreary</u> day, but <u>regardless</u>
  (A)   **(B)**   **(C)**
of the weather <u>Im</u> going to take a walk.
         (D)
<u>None of these</u>.
  (E)

16. Elaine <u>prepared</u> the entire <u>diner</u>
       (A)   **(B)**
and <u>served</u> it to her <u>guests</u>.
   (C)   **(D)**
<u>None of these</u>.
  (E)

PART IV: READING COMPREHENSION

8 Questions • 8 Minutes

READ EACH PASSAGE CAREFULLY. THEN, ON THE BASIS OF WHAT YOU HAVE READ, DECIDE WHICH OF THE POSSIBLE RESPONSES IS THE BEST ANSWER TO EACH QUESTION. YOU MAY READ THE PASSAGE AGAIN IF NECESSARY.

The bald eagle, a North American species, became the national emblem of the United States over two hundred years ago. A great many things have happened
5 to this bird since then.

A lot of controversy surrounded the choice of the bald eagle as our national symbol. Benjamin Franklin wanted the wild turkey to be our emblem. He said
10 of the bald eagle, ". . . He is a bird of bad moral character; he does not yet get his living honestly. . . . Besides, he is a rank coward. . . ."

Since those early years, the bald
15 eagle has been shot at by farmers, hunters, fishermen, and sheepherders. Fishermen thought the bird was killing too many salmon as well as other fish. Sheepherders said it was killing too many
20 ewes. The bird finally became so few in number that it gained protection under the Endangered Species Act.

It is true that the bald eagle eats a good deal of carrion, as do vultures. It
25 is also true the bird will steal kills from smaller hawks. But it is a beautiful and majestic bird. It did not ask to be chosen as our national symbol. Certainly the bird has its rightful place in nature and
30 deserves not to be shot into extinction. Besides, turkeys are funny looking and never fly over mountaintops. At present, the bald eagle population is on the rise.

17. The main theme of this passage deals with

(A) the faults of the bald eagle.

(B) what has happened to the bald eagle.

(C) the merits of the bird as being a good choice.

(D) eagle habitats and habits.

(E) the bird's rights.

18. Benjamin Franklin

(A) had the fishermen and hunters in mind.

(B) was a rank coward.

(C) believed the eagle a poor choice.

(D) was instrumental in upgrading turkeys.

(E) was a farmer and a sheepherder.

19. The bald eagle

(A) became our emblem without any appreciable debate.

(B) by human standards is something of a thief.

(C) eats dead things as its main diet.

(D) has had continuous protection.

(E) upsets nature's balance.

20. The Endangered Species Act

(A) deals with animals only.

(B) protects all birds in North and South America.

(C) was passed around 1800.

(D) protects people as well as animals.

(E) tries to keep living things from becoming extinct.

A yacht technically is a boat or ship used solely for the purpose of recreation. The noun "yacht" first came into English usage in the mid-1600s. It was derived
5 from the Dutch verb *jagen*, which means "to hunt or chase." The word was first used in a description of a sailboat, built by the Dutch East India Company, which was given as a gift to Charles I of England.
10 Charles found it most amusing to sail his 52-foot craft on the Thames, a great river in England.

It did not take long before many other British noblemen acquired their own fast
15 vessels. A fleet of swift yachts owned by the nobles led invariably to the sport of yacht racing.

The sport has survived the centuries and has become international in scope.
20 The American sailing ships have for a long time been the finest and fastest afloat. It was during colonial times that we became masters at building sailing ships.

Today the sport is still restricted to
25 the rich leisure class, for yacht racing, besides requiring the utmost sailing skill and a state-of-the-art craft, necessitates enormous quantities of money.

21. The main theme of this passage deals with
    (A) building sailboats.
    (B) how America became dominant in yacht racing.
    (C) why only the rich compete in yacht racing.
    (D) what a yacht can do.
    (E) yacht racing history.

22. A yacht is a(n)
    (A) swift commercial craft.
    (B) vessel used for sport or leisure.
    (C) racing boat—motor or sail.
    (D) English verb.
    (E) Dutch invention.

23. Yacht racing
    (A) involves expensive vessels of all types.
    (B) is restricted to the noble class.
    (C) developed during the early years of this century.
    (D) involves nations all over the world.
    (E) is open to all.

24. According to the passage, yacht racing entails
    (A) one requirement.
    (B) two requirements.
    (C) three requirements.
    (D) four requirements.
    (E) five requirements.

PART V: MATHEMATICS

12 Questions • 12 Minutes

CHOOSE THE CORRECT ANSWER FOR EACH PROBLEM.

25. The next number in the series 8, 14, 26, 50, _____ is

(A) 100

(B) 94

(C) 96

(D) 98

(E) None of the above

26. At 8.25% sales tax, what is the cost (to the nearest penny) of a camera that sells for $49.95?

(A) $4.12

(B) $54.07

(C) $58.20

(D) $55

(E) None of the above

27. The circumference of a circle is 34.54 inches. Using $\pi = 3.14$, find the radius of the circle.

(A) 11

(B) 108.5

(C) 5.5

(D) 22

(E) None of the above

28. If John received a 78, 86, 88, and 80, what mark must he receive on his next test to achieve an 85 average?

(A) 90

(B) 95

(C) 93

(D) 88

(E) None of the above

29. The average rate of walking is 4 miles per hour. At that rate, how long does it take to walk $1\frac{1}{2}$ miles?

(A) $29\frac{1}{2}$ minutes

(B) 20 minutes

(C) $22\frac{1}{2}$ minutes

(D) $37\frac{1}{2}$ minutes

(E) None of the above

30. If a person has only quarters and dimes that total $4.00, the number of quarters must NOT be equal to

(A) 12

(B) 10

(C) 14

(D) 16

(E) None of the above

31. The area of a picture 30 inches by 40 inches in square feet is approximately

(A) 100 sq ft

(B) 8 sq ft

(C) 9 sq ft

(D) $8\frac{1}{3}$ sq ft

(E) None of the above

32. On the scale of a map, $\frac{1}{2}$ inch represents 150 miles. A distance of 1,350 miles is represented by

(A) 9 inches

(B) 4.5 inches

(C) 18 inches

(D) 2.5 inches

(E) None of the above

33. A number increased by $\frac{1}{7}$ of itself equals 80. The number is

(A) 80

(B) 70

(C) 10

(D) 73

(E) None of the above

34. The ratio of 1 inch to 1 yard is

(A) $\frac{1}{1}$

(B) $\frac{1}{3}$

(C) $\frac{1}{12}$

(D) $\frac{1}{36}$

(E) None of the above

35. The next number in the series using base two is 1000, 1001, 1010, 1011,

(A) 1100

(B) 1110

(C) 1101

(D) 1111

(E) None of the above

36. If it takes 5 women 3 hours to complete 1 project, how many hours would it take 3 women to complete 10 of the same projects?

(A) 10

(B) 25

(C) 50

(D) 100

(E) 150

PART VI: ESSAY QUESTION

1 Questions • 30 Minutes

WRITE AN ESSAY ON "A SPECIAL EVENING." DESCRIBE A SPECIAL EVENT YOU WENT TO RECENTLY (IT COULD BE A FILM, A CONCERT, OR A DINNER) AND SHOW WHAT MADE IT SPECIAL.

ANSWER KEY AND EXPLANATIONS

1. B	9. C	16. B	23. D	30. D
2. D	10. D	17. B	24. C	31. D
3. D	11. D	18. C	25. D	32. B
4. D	12. B	19. B	26. B	33. B
5. A	13. D	20. E	27. C	34. D
6. B	14. C	21. E	28. C	35. A
7. B	15. D	22. B	29. V	36. C
8. B				

PART I: VOCABULARY

1. **The correct answer is (B).** *Uncanny* means "eerie."

   He had an uncanny feeling about this particular person.
   He had an eerie feeling about this particular person.

2. **The correct answer is (D).** *Squander* means "waste."

   What a way to squander your money!
   What a way to waste your money!

3. **The correct answer is (D).** *Assay* is the same as survey.

   His assay was well accepted.
   His survey was well accepted.

4. **The correct answer is (D).** *Population* means "inhabitants."

   The population of the town totaled 135,000.
   The inhabitants of the town totaled 135,000.

5. **The correct answer is (A).** *Resistance* means "opposition."

   There was great resistance to the new idea.
   There was great opposition to the new idea.

6. **The correct answer is (B).** *Plausible* is credible.

   His excuse was quite plausible.
   His excuse was quite credible.

7. **The correct answer is (B).** *Curtail* is to shorten.

   We must curtail the meeting.
   We must shorten the meeting.

8. **The correct answer is (B).** A *maneuver* is a tactic.

   That was some clever maneuver!
   That was some clever tactic!

9. **The correct answer is (C).** Something *rickety* is weak.

Be careful! That staircase is rickety.
Be careful! That staircase is weak.

10. **The correct answer is (D).** *Morality* means "virtue."

We discussed the morality of keeping a secret.
We discussed the virtue of keeping a secret.

PART II: SENTENCE COMPLETION

11. **The correct answer is (D).** *Initial* means "first."

My first response is yes before I think it through.

12. **The correct answer is (B).** *Critical* means "important."

It is important that we discover a cure.

13. **The correct answer is (D).** *Strategy* means "a plan."

The coach explained his plan to the team before the game.

PART III: GRAMMAR

14. **The correct answer is (C).** The correct spelling is <u>picnicking</u>.

15. **The correct answer is (D).** <u>Im</u> is a contraction for I am; therefore, an apostrophe is necessary, and the correct spelling is <u>I'm</u>.

16. **The correct answer is (B).** <u>Diner</u> should be <u>dinner</u>.

PART IV: READING COMPREHENSION

17. **The correct answer is (B).** The passage gives a short history of the bird.

18. **The correct answer is (C).** The second paragraph provides a quote from Ben Franklin that indicates that he thought the bird was a poor choice.

19. **The correct answer is (B).** It steals kills of smaller birds.

20. **The correct answer is (E).** This is implied in the last sentence of paragraph three.

21. **The correct answer is (E).** The article deals with how the sport developed.

22. **The correct answer is (B).** This is stated in the first sentence of the passage.

23. **The correct answer is (D).** The sport is international.

24. **The correct answer is (C).** As stated in the last sentence, yacht racing requires skill, a yacht, and lots of money.

Part V: Mathematics

25. The correct answer is (D). 8 + 6 = 14 + 12 = 26 + 24 = 50 + 48 = 98

(Note: There are other ways to find the pattern to this series. This is just one way.)

26. The correct answer is (B). 8.25% as a decimal = 0.0825. $49.95 × 0.0825 = $4.12 and $49.95 + $4.12 = $54.07.

27. The correct answer is (C). Circumference = $\pi \times d$. Substituting, we get 34.54 = 3.14 × d, or 34.54 ÷ 3.14 = d.

Therefore, $d = 11$ and the radius is $\frac{1}{2}$ of that or 5.5.

28. The correct answer is (C). 78 + 86 + 88 + 80 = 332

An average of 85 for five tests would mean a total of 85 × 5 = 425 points. Therefore, 425 − 332 = 93, the necessary mark.

29. The correct answer is (C). At 4 miles per hour, one mile takes 15 minutes and $\frac{1}{2}$ mile takes $7\frac{1}{2}$ minutes. Therefore, $15 + 7\frac{1}{2} = 22\frac{1}{2}$.

30. The correct answer is (D). Since there are both quarters and dimes, there cannot be 16 quarters because 16 quarters = $4.00, and there would be no dimes.

31. The correct answer is (D). 30 in × 40 in = area of picture

1,200 sq in = area; 144 sq in = 1 sq ft

1,200 sq in ÷ 144 = 8.333 or $8\frac{1}{3}$ sq ft

32. The correct answer is (B). If $\frac{1}{2}$ inch = 150 miles , then 1 inch = 300 miles. 1,350 miles ÷ 300 = 4.5 inches.

33. The correct answer is (B). A number + $\frac{1}{7}$ of itself = 80 $x + \frac{1}{7}x = 80$

Therefore, $1\frac{1}{7}x = 80$, or $\frac{8}{7}x = 80$; $x = 80 \div \frac{8}{7}$ or

$x \frac{80}{1} \times \frac{7}{8}$

$x = 70$

34. The correct answer is (D). 1 inch to 1 yard = 1 inch to 36 inches, or $\frac{1}{36}$, since ratios must be stated in the same unit of measure.

35. The correct answer is (A). Adding one to each number place we get:

$$\begin{array}{c} 1000 \\ +1 \\ \hline 1001 \end{array} \nearrow \begin{array}{c} 1001 \\ +1 \\ \hline 1010 \end{array} \nearrow \begin{array}{c} 1010 \\ +1 \\ \hline 1011 \end{array} \text{ therefore } \nearrow \begin{array}{c} 1011 \\ +1 \\ \hline 1100 \end{array} \text{ which is the next number}$$

36. The correct answer is (C). If 5 women need 3 hours for 1 project, then 5 × 3 units of work make 1 project, (5 × 3) × 10 units of work make 10 projects, and 150 units = 10 projects.

$$(3 \text{ women})(x \text{ hours}) = 150$$
$$3x = 150$$
$$x = 50 \text{ hours}$$

Part VI: ESSAY

An essay is a short written discussion on a particular theme or topic. There are three basic parts to a complete essay:

1. An introduction—an opening paragraph stating the theme and supporting the main idea

2. The exposition—two or three paragraphs explaining and giving examples in support of the theme

3. The conclusion—a paragraph that restates the theme and summarizes the main idea

There is no correct answer to an essay question. Teachers who are able to work with students can concentrate on teaching them how to write an essay as part of their Language Arts curriculum.

A student working on his or her own can look at the model, study its structure, and practice writing his or her own answer following the same pattern.

Remember: The essay is an important part of the exam and might mean the difference between acceptance or rejection. The following is an example of a model essay:

An Exciting Play I Saw

Introduction
main idea

    When I visited New York City last month, my parents took me to see a Broadway show.

The name of the show was *Annie*. I had never seen a live Broadway production before, and I was amazed at everything I saw

Exposition
details about
topic

    The theatre was huge and filled with excitement. There was a full orchestra right under the stage. The music was incredible. We sat right up front where you could almost touch the performers. The stage sets were beautiful and looked so real.

The children in the play seemed to work very hard, and yet they looked as if they were having fun. They sang and danced throughout. Annie had her dog on stage with her. Even he seemed to be enjoying himself.

My parents told me that a person could see many Broadway plays since performances are scheduled six times a week in the evenings and twice a week during the daytime. The daytime performances are called matinees.

Conclusion
summary of
main idea

    I will never forget that exciting evening. I hope that when I return to New York, I can see many more shows.

NOTES

NOTES